The CHOCOLATE COOKBOOK

The
CHOCOLATE
COOKBOOK

CHRISTINE FRANCE

HH
HERMES
HOUSE

Paperback edition published by Hermes House
an imprint of
Anness Publishing Limited
Hermes House
88-89 Blackfriars Road
London SE1 8HA

A CIP catalogue record for this book is available from the British Library

Publisher: Joanna Lorenz
Project Editor: Margaret Malone
Designer: Nigel Partridge
Special Photography: Don Last
Cover Design: DW Design

Also published as Chocolate Dreams

© Anness Publishing Limited 1998
Updated © 2000
1 3 5 7 9 10 8 6 4 2

NOTE
Three sets of equivalent measurements have been provided in the recipes here, in the following order:
Metric, Imperial and American. It is essential that units of measurement are not mixed within each recipe.
Where conversions result in awkward numbers, these have been rounded for convenience
but are accurate enough to produce successful results.

Previously published as part of a larger compendium, *The Ultimate Encyclopedia of Chocolate*

The authors and publishers would like to thank the following people for supplying additional recipes in the book: Catherine Atkinson, Alex Barker, Carla Capalbo, Maxine Clark, Frances Cleary, Carole Clements, Roz Denny, Nicola Diggins, Joanne Farrow, Silvana Franco, Sarah Gates, Shirley Gill, Patricia Lousada, Norma MacMillan, Sue Maggs, Sarah Maxwell, Janice Murfitt, Annie Nichols, Angela Nilsen, Louise Pickford, Katherine Richmond, Hilaire Walden, Laura Washburn, Steven Wheeler, Judy Williams, Elizabeth Wolf-Cohen.
Additional recipe photographs supplied by: Karl Adamson, Edward Allwright, David Armstrong, Steve Baxter, James Duncan, Michelle Garrett, Amanda Heywood, Tim Hill, David Jordan.

CONTENTS

INTRODUCTION   6

THE RECIPES   19

INTRODUCTION

One of the greatest treasures ever discovered was the bean from the tree *Theobroma cacao,* the original source of chocolate. Smooth in texture, intense in taste, subtly perfumed and elegant to behold, chocolate is a rich source of sensory pleasure, adored by almost everyone.

Chocolate Dreams is a celebration of this divine food, for divine it really is – translated from the Greek, *theobroma* literally means "food of the gods". Since the earliest days of its discovery, chocolate has woven intricate links among people on every imaginable level – national, cultural, social, economic and spiritual. Over the centuries it has been eagerly consumed in one form or another by all levels of society, and has initiated comment from the church, the medical profession, scientists, social reformers and royalty.

Historical records show that it was the ancient Mesoamerican civilizations living in the heart of equatorial Central America who were responsible for first cultivating the tree from which chocolate is derived. Ancient Mayan writings refer to cacao as the food

of the gods, and drawings show a drink made from cacao beans being used to solemnize sacred rituals.

Hernán Cortez, the sixteenth century Spanish explorer, is generally considered to be the first European to recognize the potential of chocolate and in 1580 the first ever chocolate-processing plant was set up in Spain. From there, it did not take long for the delights of chocolate to take a firm hold with different cultures. Once introduced into Europe, chocolate was soon transformed from bean to beverage and from beverage to confectionery, on an ever larger commercial scale. The names of some of the early manufacturers; such as the Terrys, the Cadburys and the Rowntrees, have become household names in the western world.

The bitter, greasy, cold beverage drunk by the ancient Mayans and Aztecs bears little resemblance to the deliciously smooth, rich and creamy substance that is now loved the world over. Flavourings and sweetness may vary from country to country, but what unites the different products is that smooth, sensuous, melt-in-the-mouth quality that is so hard, and so pointless, to resist. There is hardly a country in the western world that does not have chocolate as part of its culinary culture, whether it be a moist chocolate brownie from America, a chocolate-covered pancake from Hungary, or a rich, foaming cup of thick Spanish drinking chocolate.

Chocolate Dreams explores just what it is that makes chocolate so irresistible. There are over 125 recipes, covering cakes, slices, puddings and desserts, and the book's introduction includes all the essential techniques that will help you make the most of these tempting recipes. There are mouthwatering ideas for every kind of chocolate cake imaginable, from homely Marbled Chocolate-peanut Butter Cake to the decadent White Chocolate Cappuccino Gâteau. A chapter on hot desserts will devastate you with Hot Chocolate Zabaglione, Rich Chocolate Brioche Bake and Chocolate Pecan Pie. Recipes for chocolate tarts, pies and chilled desserts include classics such as Luxury White Chocolate Cheesecake and Tiramisu in Chocolate Cups; and there are plenty of recipes for biscuits and little cakes. You will also

see how to make your own chocolates and truffles, and the most deeply indulgent chocolate drinks, such as Mexican Hot Chocolate and Irish Chocolate Velvet.

Chocolate Dreams is a celebration and exploration of a wonderful food. Indulge yourself in a gastronomic chocolate feast and accept the fact that if chocolate is not already an intrinsic part of your life, this book will make sure that it becomes one.

TYPES OF CHOCOLATE

COUVERTURE (LEFT)
The professionals' choice, this is a fine-quality pure chocolate with a high percentage of cocoa butter, which gives it a high gloss. It is suitable for decorative use and for making handmade chocolates. It must generally be tempered.

PLAIN DARK CHOCOLATE (BELOW)
Often called "luxury", "bitter" or "continental" chocolate, this has a high percentage of cocoa solids – around 75 per cent – with little or no added sugar. Its rich, intense flavour and good dark colour make it an ideal ingredient in desserts and cakes.

MILK CHOCOLATE (RIGHT)
This contains powdered or condensed milk and generally around 20 per cent cocoa solids. The flavour is mild and sweet. Although this is the most popular eating chocolate, it is not as suitable as plain chocolate for melting and cooking.

PLAIN CHOCOLATE (ABOVE)
Ordinary plain chocolate is the most widely available chocolate to use in cooking. It contains anywhere between 30 per cent and 70 per cent cocoa solids, so check the label before you buy. The higher the cocoa solids, the better the chocolate flavour will be.

COCOA (LEFT)
This is made from the pure cocoa mass after most of the cocoa butter has been extracted. The mass is roasted, then ground to make a powder. It is probably the most economical way of giving puddings and baked goods a chocolate flavour.

ORGANIC CHOCOLATE (ABOVE)

This is slightly more expensive than other types of chocolate but is a quality product, high in cocoa solids, produced without pesticides and with consideration for the environment.

CHOCOLATE CHIPS (ABOVE)

These are small pieces of chocolate of uniform size. They contain fewer cocoa solids than ordinary chocolate and are available in plain dark, milk and white flavours.

CHOCOLATE-FLAVOURED CAKE COVERING (LEFT)

This is a blend of sugar, vegetable oil, cocoa and flavourings. The flavour is poor, but the high fat content makes it suitable for chocolate curls – to improve the flavour, add some plain chocolate.

CHOCOLATE POWDER (BELOW)

Chocolate powder is used in baking and for making drinks. It has lower cocoa solids than pure cocoa and has a much milder, sweeter taste.

WHITE CHOCOLATE (BELOW LEFT)

This does not contain any cocoa solids but gets its flavour from cocoa buttter. It is sweet, and the better quality white chocolate is quite rich and smooth. White chocolate must be melted with care, as it does not withstand heat as well as plain chocolate.

TECHNIQUES

MELTING CHOCOLATE

If chocolate is being melted on its own, all the equipment must be completely dry, as water may cause the chocolate to thicken and become a stiff paste. For this reason, do not cover chocolate during or after melting it, as condensation could form. If chocolate does thicken, add a little pure white vegetable fat (not butter or margarine) and mix well. If this does not work, start again. Do not discard the thickened chocolate; melt it with cream to make a sauce.

With or without liquid, chocolate should be melted very slowly. It is easily burned or scorched, and then develops a bad flavour. If any steam gets into the chocolate, it can turn into a solid mass. If this happens, stir in a little pure white vegetable fat. Dark chocolate should not be heated above 50°C/120°F. Milk and white chocolate should not be heated above 45°C/110°F. Take particular care when melting white chocolate, which clogs very easily when subjected to heat.

MELTING CHOCOLATE OVER SIMMERING WATER

<u>1</u> Chop or cut the chocolate into small pieces with a sharp knife to enable it to melt quickly and evenly.

<u>2</u> Put the chocolate in the top of a double boiler or in a heatproof bowl over a saucepan of barely simmering water. The bowl should not touch the water.

<u>3</u> Heat gently until the chocolate is melted and smooth, stirring occasionally. Remove from the heat and stir.

MELTING CHOCOLATE OVER DIRECT HEAT

When a recipe recommends melting chocolate with a liquid such as milk, cream or even butter, this can be done over direct heat in a saucepan.

<u>1</u> Choose a heavy-based saucepan. Add the chocolate and liquid and melt over a low heat, stirring frequently, until the chocolate is melted and the mixture is smooth. Remove from heat immediately. This method is also used for making sauces, icings and some sweets.

<u>2</u> Chocolate can also be melted in a very low oven. Preheat oven to 110°C/ 225°F/Gas ¼. Put the chocolate in an ovenproof bowl and place in the oven for a few minutes. Remove the chocolate before it is completely melted and stir until smooth.

MELTING CHOCOLATE IN THE MICROWAVE

Check the chocolate at frequent intervals during the cooking time. These times are for a 650–700 W oven and are approximate, as microwave ovens vary.

<u>1</u> Place 115g/4oz chopped or broken dark, bittersweet or semi-sweet chocolate in a microwave-safe bowl and microwave on Medium for about 2 minutes. The same quantity of milk or white chocolate should be melted on Low for about 2 minutes.

<u>2</u> Check the chocolate frequently during the cooking time. The chocolate will not change shape, but will start to look shiny. It must then be removed from the microwave and stirred until completely melted and smooth.

TEMPERING CHOCOLATE

TEMPERING CHOCOLATE

Tempering is the process of gently heating and cooling chocolate to stabilize the emulsification of cocoa solids and butterfat. This technique is generally used by professionals handling couverture chocolate. It allows the chocolate to shrink quickly (to allow easy release from a mould, for example with Easter eggs) or to be kept at room temperature for several weeks or months without losing its crispness and shiny surface. All solid chocolate is tempered in production, but once melted loses its "temper" and must be tempered again unless it is to be used immediately. Untempered chocolate tends to "bloom" or becomes dull and streaky or takes on a cloudy appearance. This can be avoided if the melted chocolate is put in the fridge immediately: chilling the chocolate solidifies the cocoa butter and prevents it from rising to the surface and "blooming". General baking and dessert-making do not require tempering, which is a fussy procedure and takes practice. However, it is useful to be aware of the technique when preparing sophisticated decorations, moulded chocolates or coatings. Most shapes can be made without tempering if they are chilled immediately.

EQUIPMENT

To temper chocolate successfully, you will need a marble slab or similar cool, smooth surface, such as an upturned baking sheet. A flexible plastic scraper is ideal for spreading the chocolate, but you can use a palette knife. As the temperature is crucial, you will need a chocolate thermometer. Look for this at a specialist kitchen supply shop, where you may also find blocks of tempered chocolate, ready for immediate use.

1 Break up the chocolate into small pieces and place it in the top of a double boiler or a heatproof bowl over a saucepan of hot water. Heat gently until just melted.

2 Remove from the heat. Spoon about three-quarters of the melted chocolate on to a marble slab or other cool, smooth, non-porous work surface.

3 With a flexible plastic scraper or palette knife, spread the chocolate thinly, then scoop it up before spreading it again. Repeat the sequence, keeping the chocolate constantly on the move, for about 5 minutes.

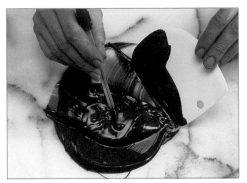

4 Using a chocolate thermometer, check the temperature of the chocolate as you work it. As soon as the temperature registers 28°C/82°F, tip the chocolate back into the bowl and stir into the remaining chocolate.

5 With the addition of the hot chocolate, the temperature should now be 32°C/90°F, making the chocolate ready for use. To test, drop a little of the chocolate from a spoon on to the marble; it should set very quickly.

STORING CHOCOLATE

Chocolate can be stored successfully for up to a year if the conditions are favourable. This means a dry place with a temperature of around 20°C/68°F. At higher temperatures, the chocolate may develop white streaks as the fat comes to the surface. Although this will not spoil the flavour, it will mar the appearance of the chocolate, making it unsuitable for use as a decoration. When storing chocolate, keep it cool and dry. Place inside an airtight container, away from strong smelling foods. Check the "best before" dates on the pack.

PIPING WITH CHOCOLATE

Pipe chocolate directly on to a cake, or on to non-stick baking paper to make run-outs, small outlined shapes or irregular designs. After melting the chocolate, allow it to cool slightly so it just coats the back of a spoon. If it still flows freely it will be too runny to hold its shape when piped. When it is the right consistency, you then need to work fast as the chocolate will set quickly. Use a paper piping bag and keep the pressure very tight, as the chocolate will flow readily without encouragement.

MAKING A PAPER PIPING BAG

A non-stick paper cone is ideal for piping small amounts of messy liquids like chocolate as it is small, easy to handle and disposable, unlike a conventional piping bag, which will need cleaning.

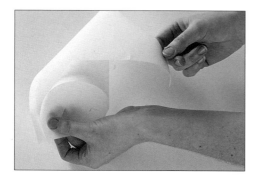

1 Fold a square of non-stick baking paper in half to form a triangle. With the triangle point facing you, fold the left corner down to the centre.

2 Fold the right corner down and wrap it around the folded left corner to form a cone. Fold the ends into the cone.

3 Spoon the melted chocolate into the cone and fold the top edges over. When ready to pipe, snip off the end of the point neatly to make a tiny hole, about 3 mm/$\frac{1}{8}$ in in diameter.

4 Another method is to use a small heavy-duty freezer or plastic bag. Place a piping nozzle in one corner of the bag, so that it is in the correct position for piping. Fill as above, squeezing the filling into one corner and twisting the top to seal. Snip off the corner of the bag, if necessary, so that the tip of the nozzle emerges, and squeeze gently to pipe the design.

CHOCOLATE DRIZZLES

You can have great fun making random shapes or, with a steady hand, special designs that will look great on cakes or biscuits.

1 Melt the chocolate and pour it into a paper cone or small piping bag fitted with a very small plain nozzle. Drizzle the chocolate on to a baking sheet lined with non-stick baking paper to make small, self-contained lattice shapes, such as circles or squares. Allow to set for 30 minutes then peel off the paper.

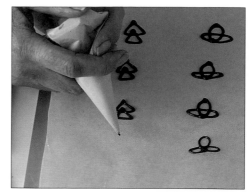

2 Chocolate can be used in many designs, such as flowers or butterflies. Use non-stick baking paper as tracing paper and pipe the chocolate over the chosen design or decorative shape.

3 For butterflies, pipe chocolate on to individually cut squares and leave until just beginning to set. Use a long, thin box (such as an egg carton) and place the butterfly shape in the box or between the cups so it is bent in the centre, creating the butterfly shape. Chill until needed.

PIPING ON TO CAKES

This looks effective on top of a cake iced with coffee glacé icing.

1 Melt 50g/2oz each of white and plain dark chocolate in separate bowls, and allow to cool slightly. Place the chocolates in separate paper piping bags. Cut a small piece off the pointed end of each bag in a straight line.

2 Hold each piping bag in turn above the surface of the cake and pipe the chocolates all over as shown in the picture. Alternatively, pipe a freehand design in one continuous curvy line, first with one bag of chocolate, then the other.

PIPING CURLS

Make lots of these curly shapes and store them in a cool place ready for using as cake decorations. Try piping the lines in contrasting colours of chocolate to vary the effect.

1 Melt 115g/4oz chocolate and allow to cool slightly. Cover a rolling pin with baking parchment and attach it with tape. Fill a paper piping bag with the chocolate and cut a small piece off the pointed end in a straight line.

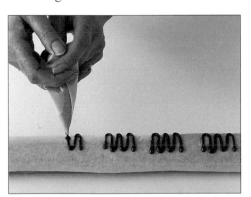

2 Pipe lines of chocolate backwards and forwards over the baking parchment.

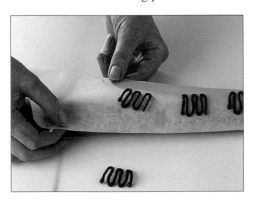

3 Leave the piped curls to set in a cool place, then carefully peel off the baking parchment. Use a palette knife to lift the curls on to the cake.

FEATHERING OR MARBLING CHOCOLATE

These two related techniques provide some of the easiest and most effective ways of decorating the top of a cake, and they are also used when making a swirled mixture for cut-outs. Chocolate sauce and double cream can also be feathered or marbled to decorate a dessert.

1 Melt two contrasting colours of chocolate and spread one over the cake or surface to be decorated.

2 Spoon the contrasting chocolate into a piping bag and pipe lines or swirls over the chocolate base.

3 Working quickly before the chocolate sets, draw a skewer or cocktail stick through the swirls to create a feathered or marbled effect.

CHOCOLATE RUN-OUTS

Try piping the outline in one colour of chocolate and filling in the middle with another. The effect can be dramatic.

1 Tape a piece of greaseproof paper to a baking sheet or flat board. Draw around a shaped biscuit cutter on to the paper several times. Secure a piece of non-stick baking paper over the top.

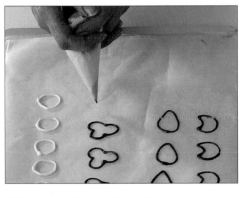

2 Pipe over the outline of your design in a continuous thread.

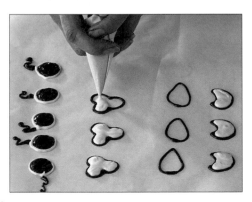

3 Cut the end off the other bag, making the hole slightly wider than before, and pipe the chocolate to fill in the outline so it looks slightly rounded. Leave the shapes to set in a cool place, then carefully lift them off the non-stick baking paper with a palette knife.

CHOCOLATE DECORATIONS

GRATED CHOCOLATE

Chocolate can be grated by hand or in a food processor. Make sure you grate it at the correct temperature.

<u>1</u> Chill the chocolate and hold it with a piece of folded foil or paper towel to prevent the heat of your hand melting it. Hold a hand- or box-grater over a large plate and grate with an even pressure.

<u>2</u> A food processor fitted with the metal blade can also be used to grate chocolate, but be sure the chocolate is soft enough to be pierced with a sharp knife. Cut the chocolate into small pieces and, with the machine running, drop the chocolate pieces through the feeder tube until very fine shavings are produced. Use the grater attachment and pusher to feed the chocolate through the processor for larger shavings.

COOK'S TIPS
The chocolate you use for decorating should not be too cold or it will splinter; warm chocolate will give a softer, looser curl, but do not allow it to become too soft or warm or it will be difficult to handle and may bloom. Use tempered chocolate for the best results.

COOK'S TIPS
If using a metal grater for grating chocolate, chill it in the freezer before use and the chocolate will be less likely to melt.
Experiment with different utensils when making chocolate curls. Metal palette knives, paint scrapers, tablespoons and even wide, straight pastry scrapers can be used.

MINI CHOCOLATE CURLS

Chocolate curls make an ideal decoration for many desserts and cakes, whether these are made from plain, bittersweet or white chocolate. These curls can be made very quickly using a vegetable peeler, and can be stored for several weeks in an airtight container in a cool, dry place.

<u>1</u> Bring a thick piece or bar of chocolate to room temperature. (Chocolate that is too cold will "grate", or if too warm will slice.) With a swivel-bladed peeler held over a plate or baking sheet, pull the blade firmly along the edge of the chocolate and allow curls to fall on to the plate or baking sheet in a single layer.

<u>2</u> Use a skewer or cocktail stick to transfer curls to the dessert or cake.

CHUNKY CHOCOLATE·CURLS

These curls are best made with dark chocolate that has been melted with pure white vegetable fat (about 5ml/1tsp per 25g/1oz of chocolate), which keeps the chocolate from hardening completely.

<u>1</u> Melt 175g/6oz plain or bittersweet chocolate with 30ml/2tbsp pure white vegetable fat, stirring until smooth. Pour into a small rectangular or square tin lined with foil or non-stick baking paper to produce a block about 2.5cm/1in thick. Chill until set.

<u>2</u> Allow the block to come to room temperature, remove it from the tin, then hold it with a piece of folded foil or paper towel (to stop it melting) and use a swivel-bladed peeler to produce short chunky curls. The block of chocolate can also be grated.

COOK'S TIPS
The decorations on this page are useful for all kinds of cakes and desserts. When you have mastered the techniques, try marbling dark and white chocolate together for a special effect.

CHOCOLATE SCROLLS OR SHORT ROUND CURLS

Temper dark or white chocolate, or use chocolate prepared for Chunky Chocolate Curls to produce these scrolls.

1 Pour the prepared chocolate evenly on to a marble slab or the back of a baking sheet. Using a metal palette knife, spread to about 3mm/⅛in thick and allow to set for about 30 minutes until just firm.

2 To make long scrolls, use the blade of a long, sharp knife on the surface of the chocolate, and, with both hands, push away from your body at a 25–45° angle to scrape off a thin layer of chocolate. Twist the handle of the knife about a quarter of a circle to make a slightly wider scroll. Use a teaspoon to make cup-shaped curls.

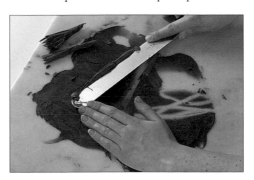

3 A variety of shapes and sizes can be produced, depending on the temperature of the chocolate and the tool used.

CHOCOLATE SQUIGGLES

Melt a quantity of chocolate and spread fairly thinly over a cool, smooth surface, leave until just set, then draw a citrus zester firmly across the surface to remove curls or "squiggles" of the chocolate.

CHOCOLATE CUT-OUTS

You can make abstract shapes, or circles, squares and diamonds, by cutting them out free-hand with a sharp knife.

1 Cover a baking sheet with baking parchment and tape down at each corner. Melt 115g/4 oz dark, milk or white chocolate. Pour the chocolate on to the baking parchment.

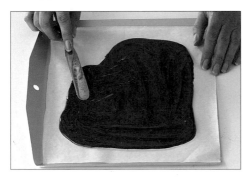

2 Spread the chocolate evenly with a palette knife. Allow to stand until the surface is firm enough to cut, but not so hard that it will break. It should no longer feel sticky when touched lightly with your finger.

3 Press the cutter firmly through the chocolate and lift off the paper with a palette knife. Try not to touch the surface of the chocolate or you will leave marks on it and spoil its appearance.

4 The finished shapes can be left plain or piped with a contrasting chocolate for a decorative effect.

5 Abstract shapes can be cut with a knife free-hand. They look particularly effective pressed on to the sides of a cake iced with plain or chocolate buttercream.

COOK'S TIPS

If you do not feel confident about cutting chocolate cut-outs freehand, use biscuit or aspic cutters. Cut-outs look good around the sides of cakes or gâteaux. Space them at regular intervals or allow them to overlap.

CHOCOLATE LEAVES

You can use any fresh, non-toxic leaf with distinct veins, to make these decorations. Rose, bay or lemon leaves work well. If small leaves are required, for decorating petits fours, for instance, use mint or lemon balm leaves.

1 Wash and dry the leaves thoroughly. Melt plain or white chocolate and use a pastry brush or spoon to coat the veined side of each leaf completely.

2 Place the coated leaves chocolate-side up on a baking sheet lined with non-stick baking paper to set.

3 Starting at the stem end, gently peel away each leaf in turn. Store the chocolate leaves in a cool place until needed.

CHOCOLATE BASKETS

These impressive baskets make pretty, edible containers for mousse, or ice cream.

MAKES 6

*175g/6oz plain, milk or white chocolate
25g/1oz/2 tbsp butter*

1 Cut out six 15cm/6in rounds from non-stick baking paper.

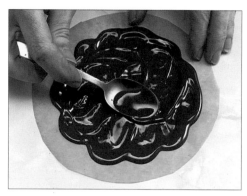

2 Melt the chocolate with the butter in a heatproof bowl over barely simmering water. Stir until smooth. Spoon one-sixth of the chocolate over each round, using a teaspoon to spread it to within 2cm/¾in of the edge.

BELOW: Chocolate baskets can be used to hold many kinds of delicious desserts, such as mousse, ice cream and tiramisu.

3 Carefully lift each covered paper round and drape it over an upturned cup or ramekin, curving the edges to create a frilled effect.

4 Leave until completely set, then carefully lift off the chocolate shape and peel away the paper.

5 For a different effect, brush the chocolate over, leaving the edges jagged. Invert chocolate baskets on individual dessert plates and gently peel off the paper. Add your chosen filling, taking care not to break the chocolate.
6 For a simple filling, whip cream with a little orange-flavoured liqueur, pipe the mixture in swirls in the chocolate cups and top with mandarin segments, half-dipped in chocolate.

CHOCOLATE CUPS

Large or small cupcake papers or sweet cases can be used to make chocolate cups to fill with ice cream, mousse or liqueur. Use double liners inside each other for extra support.

1 Melt the chocolate. Using a paintbrush or pastry brush, completely coat the bottom and sides of the paper cases. Allow to set, then repeat once or twice to build up the layers. Allow to set for several hours or overnight.

2 Carefully peel off the paper case, set the chocolate cups on a baking sheet and fill as desired.

CHOCOLATE SHORTCRUST PASTRY (1)

Suitable for sweet flans and tarts, this quantity will line a 23cm/9in flan tin.

*115g/4oz plain chocolate, broken into
squares
225g/8oz/2 cups plain flour
115g/4oz/½ cup unsalted butter
15–30ml/1–2 tbsp cold water*

1 Melt the chocolate in a heatproof bowl over hot water. Remove from the heat and allow to cool, but not set.

2 Place the flour in a mixing bowl. Rub in the butter until the mixture resembles fine breadcrumbs.

3 Make a well in the centre of the rubbed-in mixture. Add the cooled chocolate and mix in together with just enough cold water to mix to a firm dough. Knead lightly, then wrap in clear film and chill before rolling out. Once you have chilled the flan tin, chill again before baking.

LEFT: These tiny chocolate cups are ideal as a container for sweets. You can also fill them with nuts and fruit for petits fours. Look out for different sizes of cases for these little cups.

CHOCOLATE SHORTCRUST PASTRY (2)

An alternative sweet chocolate pastry, this time made with cocoa. Use a 23cm/9in flan tin.

*175g/6oz/1½ cups plain flour
30ml/2 tbsp cocoa powder
30ml/2 tbsp icing sugar
115g/4oz/½ cup butter
15–30ml/1–2 tbsp cold water*

1 Sift the flour, cocoa powder and icing sugar into a mixing bowl.
2 Place the butter in a pan with the water and heat gently until just melted. Cool.
3 Stir into the flour to make a smooth dough. Chill until firm, then roll out and use as required.

TIPS FOR COOKING WITH CHOCOLATE

Melt chocolate slowly, as overheating will spoil both the flavour and texture.
Avoid overheating – dark chocolate should not be heated above 49°C/120°F; milk and white chocolate should not be heated above 43°C/110°F.
Never allow water or steam to come into contact with melting chocolate, as this may cause it to stiffen. If the chocolate comes into contact with steam, and forms a solid mass, add a small amount of pure vegetable oil and mix in. If this does not work you will have to start again. Don't discard spoiled chocolate, it will probably melt when added to another ingredient such as milk, butter or cream.
Remember to use high quality chocolate for the best results.
Look for the cocoa solid content on the back of the wrapper.
Do not cover chocolate after melting, as condensation could cause it to stiffen.

THE
RECIPES

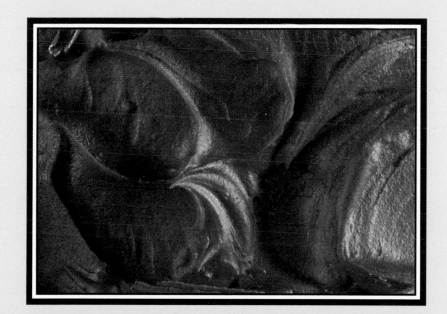

TEA-TIME CHOCOLATE TREATS

SIMPLE CHOCOLATE CAKE

2 Cream the butter or margarine with the sugar in a mixing bowl until pale and fluffy. Add the eggs one at a time, beating well after each addition. Stir in the chocolate mixture until well combined.

3 Sift the flour and cocoa over the mixture and fold in with a metal spoon until evenly mixed. Scrape into the prepared tins, smooth level and bake for 35–40 minutes or until well risen and firm. Turn out on to wire racks to cool.

4 Sandwich the cake layers together with a thick, even layer of chocolate buttercream. Dust with a mixture of icing sugar and cocoa just before serving.

SERVES 6–8

*115g/4oz plain chocolate, chopped into
small pieces
45ml/3 tbsp milk
150g/5oz/⅔ cup unsalted butter or
margarine, softened
150g/5oz/scant 1 cup light muscovado sugar
3 eggs
200g/7oz/1¾ cups self-raising flour
15ml/1 tbsp cocoa powder
1 quantity Chocolate Buttercream, for the
filling
icing sugar and cocoa powder, for dusting*

1 Preheat oven to 180°C/350°F/Gas 4. Grease two 18 cm/7 in round sandwich cake tins and line the base of each with non-stick baking paper. Select a small saucepan and a heatproof bowl that will fit over it. Place the chocolate and the milk in the bowl. Bring a small saucepan of water to just below simmering point. Place the bowl containing the chocolate mixture on top. Leave for about 5 minutes, until the chocolate softens, then stir until smooth. Leave the bowl over the saucepan, but remove from the heat.

ONE-MIX CHOCOLATE SPONGE

SERVES 8–10

175g / 6oz / ¾ cup soft margarine, at room temperature
115g / 4oz / ½ cup caster sugar
60ml / 4 tbsp golden syrup
175g / 6oz / 1½ cups self-raising flour, sifted
30ml / 2 tbsp cocoa powder, sifted
2.5ml / ½ tsp salt
3 eggs, beaten
little milk (optional)
150ml / ¼ pint / ⅔ cup whipping cream
15–30ml / 1–2 tbsp finely shredded marmalade
sifted icing sugar, to decorate

1 Preheat the oven to 180°C / 350°F / Gas 4. Grease two 18 mm / 7 in sandwich cake tins. Cream the margarine, sugar, syrup, flour, cocoa, salt and eggs in a bowl.

2 If the mixture seems a little thick, stir in enough milk to give a soft dropping consistency. Spoon the mixture into the prepared tins, and bake for about 30 minutes, changing shelves if necessary after 15 minutes, until just firm and springy to the touch.

3 Leave the cakes to cool for 5 minutes, then remove from the tins and leave to cool completely on a wire rack.

4 Whip the cream and fold in the marmalade. Use the mixture to sandwich the two cakes together. Sprinkle the top with sifted icing sugar.

Chocolate and Beetroot Layer Cake

Serves 10–12

cocoa powder, for dusting
225g/8oz can cooked whole beetroot, drained and juice reserved
115g/4oz/½ cup unsalted butter, softened
425g/15oz/2½ cups soft light brown sugar
3 eggs
15ml/1 tbsp vanilla essence
75g/3oz bittersweet chocolate, melted
225g/8oz/2 cups plain flour
10ml/2 tsp baking powder
2.5ml/½ tsp salt
120ml/4fl oz/½ cup buttermilk
chocolate curls (optional)

Chocolate Ganache Frosting

475ml/16fl oz/2 cups whipping cream or double cream
500g/1¼lb fine quality, bittersweet or plain chocolate, chopped into small pieces
15ml/1 tbsp vanilla essence

1 Preheat the oven to 180°C/350°F/ Gas 4. Grease two 23 cm/9 in cake tins and dust the base and sides with cocoa. Grate the beetroot and add to the juice. Set aside. With a hand-held electric mixer, beat the butter, brown sugar, eggs and vanilla essence in a mixing bowl until pale. Reduce the speed and beat in the melted chocolate. Sift the flour, baking powder and salt into a bowl.

2 With the mixer on low speed gradually beat the flour mixture into the butter mixture, alternately with the buttermilk. Add the beetroot and juice and beat for 1 minute. Divide between the tins and bake for 30–35 minutes or until a cake tester inserted in the centre of each cake comes out clean. Cool for 10 minutes, then turn the cakes out on a wire rack and cool completely.

3 To make the ganache frosting, heat the cream in a heavy-based saucepan over medium heat, until it just begins to boil, stirring occasionally to prevent it from scorching. Remove from the heat and stir in the chocolate, stirring constantly until melted and smooth. Stir in the vanilla essence. Strain into a bowl. Cool, then chill, stirring every 10 minutes for about 1 hour, until spreadable.

4 Assemble the cake. Place one layer on a serving plate and spread with one-third of the ganache frosting. Place the second layer on top and spread the remaining ganache over the cake, taking it down the sides. Decorate with the chocolate curls, if using. Allow the ganache frosting to set for 20–30 minutes, then chill the cake before serving.

FRENCH CHOCOLATE CAKE

SERVES 10

*250g / 9oz bittersweet chocolate, chopped into
small pieces
225g / 8oz / 1 cup unsalted butter, cut into
small pieces
90g / 3½oz / scant ½ cup granulated sugar
30ml / 2 tbsp brandy or orange-flavoured
liqueur
5 eggs
15ml / 1tbsp plain flour
icing sugar, for dusting
whipped or soured cream, for serving*

<u>1</u> Preheat oven to 180°C/350°F/Gas 4.
Generously grease a 23 x 5 cm/9 x 2 in
springform tin. Line the base with non-
stick baking paper and grease. Wrap the
bottom and sides of the tin in foil to
prevent water from seeping through into
the cake.

<u>2</u> In a saucepan, over a low heat, melt the
chocolate, butter and sugar, stirring
frequently until smooth. Remove from
the heat, cool slightly and stir in the
brandy or liqueur.

<u>3</u> In a large bowl beat the eggs lightly for
1 minute. Beat in the flour, then slowly
beat in the chocolate mixture until well
blended. Pour into the tin.

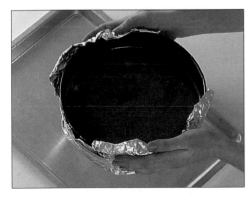

<u>4</u> Place the springform tin in a large
roasting tin. Add enough boiling water to
come 2 cm/¾ in up the side of the
springform tin. Bake for 25–30 minutes,
until the edge of the cake is set but the
centre is still soft. Remove the
springform tin from the roasting tin and
remove the foil. Cool on a wire rack. The
cake will sink in the centre and become
its classic slim shape as it cools. Don't
worry if the surface cracks slightly.

<u>5</u> Remove the side of the springform tin
and turn the cake on to a wire rack. Lift
off the springform tin base and then
carefully peel back the paper, so the base
of the cake is now the top. Leave the cake
on the rack until it is quite cold.

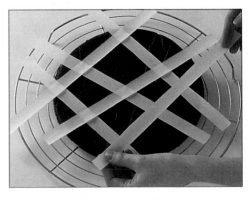

<u>6</u> Cut 6–8 strips of non-stick baking
paper 2.5 cm/1 in wide and place
randomly over the cake. Dust the cake
with icing sugar, then carefully remove
the paper. Slide the cake on to a plate and
serve with whipped or soured cream.

Caribbean Chocolate Ring with Rum Syrup

Serves 8–10

115g/4oz/½ cup unsalted butter
115g/4oz/¾ cup light muscovado sugar
2 eggs, beaten
2 ripe bananas, mashed
30ml/2 tbsp desiccated coconut
30ml/2 tbsp soured cream
115g/4oz/1 cup self-raising flour
45ml/3 tbsp cocoa powder
2.5ml/½ tsp bicarbonate of soda

For the Syrup

115g/4oz/½ cup caster sugar
30ml/2 tbsp dark rum
50g/2oz plain dark chocolate, chopped

To Decorate

mixture of tropical fruits, such as mango,
pawpaw, starfruit and cape gooseberries
chocolate shapes or curls

1 Preheat oven to 180°C/350°F/Gas 4. Grease a 1.5 litre/2½ pint/6¼ cup ring tin with butter.

2 Cream the butter and sugar in a bowl until light and fluffy. Add the eggs gradually, beating well, then mix in the bananas, coconut and soured cream.

3 Sift the flour, cocoa and bicarbonate of soda over the mixture and fold in thoroughly and evenly.

4 Tip into the prepared tin and spread evenly. Bake for 45–50 minutes, until firm to the touch. Cool for 10 minutes in the tin, then turn out to finish cooling on a wire rack.

5 For the syrup, place the sugar in a small pan. Add 60ml/4 tbsp water and heat gently, stirring occasionally until dissolved. Bring to the boil and boil rapidly, without stirring, for 2 minutes. Remove from the heat.

6 Add the rum and chocolate to the syrup and stir until the mixture is melted and smooth, then spoon evenly over the top and sides of the cake.

7 Decorate the ring with tropical fruits and chocolate shapes or curls.

CHOCOLATE AND ORANGE ANGEL CAKE

SERVES 10

25g / 1oz / ¼ cup plain flour
30ml / 2 tbsp cocoa powder
30ml / 2 tbsp cornflour
pinch of salt
5 egg whites
2.5ml / ½ tsp cream of tartar
115g / 4oz / ½ cup caster sugar
blanched and shredded rind of 1 orange,
to decorate

FOR THE ICING

200g / 7oz / scant 1 cup caster sugar
75ml / 5 tbsp cold water
1 egg white

1 Preheat oven to 180°C/350°F/Gas 4. Sift the flour, cocoa, cornflour and salt together three times. Beat the egg whites in a large bowl until foamy. Add the cream of tartar to the egg whites and whisk until soft peaks form.

2 Add the caster sugar to the egg whites a spoonful at a time, whisking after each addition. Add, by sifting, a third of the flour and cocoa mixture, and gently fold in. Repeat, sifting and folding in the flour and cocoa two more times. Spoon the mixture into a 20 cm/8 in non-stick ring tin and level the top. Bake for 35 minutes or until springy when lightly pressed. When cooled, turn upside-down on to a wire rack and leave to cool in the tin.

3 Make the icing. Put the sugar in a pan with the water. Stir over a low heat until dissolved. Boil until the syrup reaches a temperature of 120°C/250°F on a sugar thermometer, or when a drop of the syrup makes a soft ball when dropped into a cup of cold water. Remove the pan from the heat. Ease the cake out of the tin.

4 Whisk the egg white until stiff. Add the syrup in a thin stream, whisking all the time. Continue to whisk until the mixture is very thick and fluffy. Spread the icing over the top and sides of the cooled cake. Sprinkle the orange rind over the top of the cake and transfer it to a platter. Serve.

CHOCOLATE AND CHERRY POLENTA CAKE

SERVES 8

50g / 2oz / ⅓ cup quick-cook polenta
200g / 7oz plain chocolate, chopped into
small pieces
5 eggs, separated
175g / 6oz / ¾ cup caster sugar
115g / 4oz / 1 cup ground almonds
75ml / 5 tbsp plain flour
finely grated rind of 1 orange
115g / 4oz / 1 cup glacé cherries, halved
icing sugar, for dusting

1 Place the polenta in a heatproof bowl and pour over just enough boiling water to cover (about 120ml / 4 fl oz / ½ cup). Stir well, then cover the bowl and leave to stand for about 30 minutes, until the quick-cook polenta has absorbed all the excess moisture.

2 Preheat oven to 190°C / 375°F / Gas 5. Grease a deep 22 cm / 8½ in round cake tin and line the base with non-stick baking paper. Melt the chocolate.

3 Whisk the egg yolks with the sugar in a bowl until thick and pale. Beat in the chocolate, then fold in the polenta, ground almonds, flour and orange rind.

4 Whisk the egg whites in a grease-free bowl until stiff. Stir about 15ml / 1 tbsp of the whites into the chocolate mixture to lighten it, then fold in the rest. Finally, fold in the cherries. Scrape the mixture into the prepared tin and bake for 45–55 minutes or until well risen and firm. Turn out and cool on a wire rack, then dust with icing sugar to serve.

MARBLED CHOCOLATE-PEANUT BUTTER CAKE

SERVES 12–14

115g/4oz bittersweet chocolate, chopped into
small pieces
225g/8oz/1 cup unsalted butter, softened
225g/8oz/⅔ cup smooth or chunky
peanut butter
200g/7oz/scant 1 cup granulated sugar
225g/8 oz/1¼ cups soft light brown sugar
5 eggs
225g/8 oz/2 cups plain flour
10ml/2 tsp baking powder
2.5ml/½ tsp salt
120ml/4fl oz/½ cup milk
50g/2oz/⅓ cup chocolate chips

CHOCOLATE PEANUT BUTTER GLAZE

25g/1oz/2 tbsp butter, cut up
30ml/2 tbsp smooth peanut butter
45ml/3 tbsp golden syrup
5ml/1 tsp vanilla essence
175g/6oz plain chocolate, chopped into
small pieces
15ml/1 tbsp water

1 Preheat oven to 180°C/350°F/Gas 4.
Generously grease and flour a 3 litre/
5 pint/12 cup tube or ring tin. Melt
the chocolate. In a large mixing bowl beat
the butter, peanut butter and sugars until
light and creamy. Add the eggs one at a
time, beating well after each addition.
2 In a medium bowl, sift together the
flour, baking powder and salt. Add to the
butter mixture alternately with the milk
until just blended. Pour half the mixture
into another bowl. Stir the melted
chocolate into one bowl of batter until
well blended. Stir the chocolate chips
into the other bowl of batter.

3 Using a large spoon, drop alternate
spoonfuls of chocolate mixture and
peanut butter mixture into the prepared
tin. Using a knife, pull through the
batters to create a swirled marbled effect.
Bake for 50–60 minutes, until the top
springs back when touched. Cool the
cake in the tin for 10 minutes. Turn out
on to a rack to cool completely.

4 Make the glaze. Combine all the
ingredients in a small saucepan. Melt over
a low heat, stirring until well blended and
smooth. Cool slightly. When slightly
thickened, drizzle the glaze over the cake,
allowing it to run down the sides.

CHOCOLATE-ORANGE BATTENBURG

3 Fold the rest of the flour and the cocoa into the remaining bowl of mixture, with sufficient milk to give a soft dropping consistency. Fill one half of the tin with the orange mixture and the second half with the chocolate. Flatten the top with a wetted spoon. Bake for 15 minutes, then reduce the heat to 160°C/325°F/Gas 3, and bake the cake for a further 20–30 minutes or until the top is just firm. Leave to cool in the tin for a few minutes. Turn out the cakes on to a board and cut each one into two identical strips. Trim so that they are even, then leave to cool.

4 Using the chocolate and nut spread, sandwich the cakes together, chocolate and orange side by side, then orange and chocolate on top. Spread the sides with more of the chocolate and nut spread. On a board lightly dusted with cornflour, roll out the white almond paste to a rectangle 18 cm/7 in wide and long enough to wrap all around the cake. Wrap the almond paste carefully around the cake, making the join underneath. Press to seal. Mark a criss-cross pattern on the almond paste with a knife, then pinch together the corners if desired. Store in a cool place. Cut with a sharp knife into chequered slices to serve.

SERVES 8

115g/4oz/½ cup soft margarine
115g/4oz/½ cup caster sugar
2 eggs, beaten
few drops of vanilla essence
115g/4oz/1 cup ground almonds
115g/4oz/1 cup self-raising flour, sifted
grated rind and juice of ½ orange
30ml/2 tbsp cocoa powder, sifted
30 15ml/2 3 tbsp milk
1 jar chocolate and nut spread
cornflour, to dust
225g/8oz white almond paste

1 Preheat oven to 180°C/350°F/Gas 4. Grease and line an 18 cm/7 in square cake tin. Arrange a double piece of foil across the middle of the tin, to divide it into two equal rectangles.

2 Cream the margarine and sugar in a mixing bowl, then beat in the eggs, vanilla essence and ground almonds. Divide the mixture evenly between two bowls. Fold half the flour into one bowl, then stir in the orange rind and sufficient juice to give a soft dropping consistency. Set the orange-flavoured mixture aside.

CHOCOLATE CHIP WALNUT LOAF

MAKES 1 LOAF

115g/4oz/½ cup caster sugar
115g/4oz/1 cup plain flour
5ml/1 tsp baking powder
60ml/4 tbsp cornflour
115g/4oz/½ cup butter, softened
2 eggs, beaten
5ml/1 tsp vanilla essence
30ml/2 tbsp currants or raisins
25g/1oz/¼ cup walnuts, finely chopped
grated rind of ½ lemon
45ml/3 tbsp plain chocolate chips
icing sugar, for dusting

1 Preheat oven to 180°C/350°F/Gas 4. Grease and line a 22 x 12 cm/8½ x 4½ in loaf tin. Sprinkle 25ml/1½ tbsp of the caster sugar into the pan and tilt to distribute the sugar in an even layer over the bottom and sides. Shake out any excess sugar.

2 Sift the flour, baking powder and cornflour into a mixing bowl. Repeat this twice more. Set aside.

3 With an electric mixer, cream the butter until soft. Add the remaining sugar and continue beating until light and fluffy. Add the eggs, one at a time, beating after each addition.

4 Gently fold the dry ingredients into the butter mixture, in three batches; do not overmix.

5 Fold in the vanilla essence, currants or raisins, walnuts, lemon rind and chocolate chips until just blended.

6 Pour the mixture into the prepared tin and bake for 45–50 minutes. Cool in the tin for 5 minutes before transferring to a rack to cool completely. Place on a serving plate and dust over an even layer of icing sugar before serving. Alternatively, top with glacé icing and decorate with walnut halves.

BITTER MARMALADE CHOCOLATE LOAF

SERVES 8

*115g/4oz plain chocolate, chopped into
small pieces
3 eggs
200g/7oz/scant 1 cup caster sugar
175ml/6fl oz/¾ cup soured cream
200g/7oz/1¾ cups self-raising flour*

FOR THE FILLING AND GLAZE

*175g/6oz/⅔ cup bitter orange marmalade
115g/4oz plain chocolate, chopped into
small pieces
60ml/4 tbsp soured cream
shredded orange rind, to decorate*

1 Preheat oven to 180°C/350°F/Gas 4. Grease a 900g/2lb loaf tin lightly, then line it with non-stick baking paper. Melt the chocolate.

2 Combine the eggs and sugar in a mixing bowl. Using a hand-held electric mixer, whisk the mixture until it is thick and creamy, then stir in the soured cream and chocolate. Fold in the self-raising flour evenly, using a metal spoon and a figure-of-eight action.

3 Scrape the mixture into the prepared tin and bake for about 1 hour or until well risen and firm to the touch. Cool for a few minutes in the tin, then turn out on to a wire rack and leave the loaf to cool completely.

4 Make the filling. Spoon two-thirds of the marmalade into a small saucepan and melt over a gentle heat. Melt the chocolate and stir it into the marmalade with the soured cream.

5 Slice the cake across into three layers and sandwich back together with about half the marmalade filling. Spread the rest over the top of the cake and leave to set. Spoon the remaining marmalade over the cake and scatter with shredded orange rind, to decorate.

CHOCOLATE CHIP MARZIPAN LOAF

MAKES 1 LOAF

115g / 4oz / ½ cup unsalted butter, softened
150g / 5oz / scant 1 cup light muscovado sugar
2 eggs, beaten
45ml / 3 tbsp cocoa powder
150g / 5oz / 1¼ cups self-raising flour
130g / 3½ oz marzipan
60ml / 4 tbsp plain chocolate chips

1 Preheat oven to 180°C/350°F/Gas 4. Grease a 900g/2lb loaf tin and line the base with non-stick baking paper. Cream the butter and sugar in a mixing bowl until light and fluffy.

2 Add the eggs to the creamed mixture one at a time, beating well after each addition to combine.

3 Sift the cocoa and flour over the mixture and fold in evenly.

4 Chop the marzipan into small pieces with a sharp knife. Tip into a bowl and mix with the chocolate chips. Set aside about 60ml/4 tbsp and fold the rest evenly into the cake mixture.

5 Scrape the mixture into the prepared tin, level the top and scatter with the reserved marzipan and chocolate chips.

6 Bake for 45–50 minutes or until the loaf is risen and firm. Cool for a few minutes in the tin, then turn out on to a wire rack to cool completely.

CHOCOLATE COCONUT ROULADE

4 Scrape the mixture into the prepared tin, taking it right into the corners. Smooth the surface with a palette knife, then bake for 20–25 minutes or until well risen and springy to the touch.

5 Turn the cooked roulade out on to the sugar-dusted greaseproof paper and carefully peel off the lining paper. Cover with a damp, clean dish towel and leave to cool completely.

6 Make the filling. Whisk the cream with the whisky in a bowl until the mixture just holds it shape, grate the creamed coconut and stir in with the sugar.

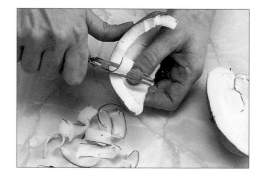

SERVES 8

115g / 4oz / ½ cup caster sugar
5 eggs, separated
50g / 2oz / ½ cup cocoa powder
FOR THE FILLING
300ml / ½ pint / 1¼ cups double cream
45ml / 3 tbsp whisky
or brandy
50g / 2oz piece solid creamed coconut
30ml / 2 tbsp caster sugar
FOR THE TOPPING
a piece of fresh coconut
dark chocolate for curls

1 Preheat oven to 180°C / 350°F / Gas 4. Grease a 33 x 23 cm / 13 x 9 in Swiss roll tin. Lay a large sheet of greaseproof paper or non-stick baking paper on the work surface and dust it evenly with 30ml / 2 tbsp of the caster sugar.

2 Place the egg yolks in a heatproof bowl. Add the remaining caster sugar and whisk with a hand-held electric mixer until the mixture is thick enough to leave a trail. Sift the cocoa over, then fold in carefully and evenly with a metal spoon.

3 Whisk the egg whites in a clean, grease-free bowl until they form soft peaks. Fold about 15ml / 1 tbsp of the whites into the chocolate mixture to lighten it, then fold in the rest evenly.

7 Uncover the sponge and spread about three-quarters of the cream mixture to the edges. Roll up carefully from a long side. Transfer to a plate, pipe or spoon the remaining cream mixture on top. Use a vegetable peeler to make coconut and chocolate curls and pile on the cake.

CHOCOLATE CHESTNUT ROULADE

SERVES 10–12

*175g/6oz bittersweet chocolate, chopped into
small pieces*
30ml/2 tbsp cocoa powder, sifted
60ml/4 tbsp hot strong coffee or espresso
6 eggs, separated
75g/3oz/6 tbsp caster sugar
pinch of cream of tartar
5ml/1 tsp pure vanilla essence
cocoa powder, for dusting
glacé chestnuts, to decorate

CHESTNUT CREAM FILLING

475ml/16fl oz/2 cups double cream
30ml/2 tbsp rum or coffee-flavoured liqueur
*350g/12oz/1½ cups canned sweetened
chestnut purée*
115g/4oz bittersweet chocolate, grated

1 Preheat oven to 180°C/350°F/Gas 4.
Lightly grease the base and sides of a
39 x 27 x 2.5 cm/15½ x 10½ x 1 in Swiss
roll tin. Line with non-stick baking paper,
allowing a 2.5 cm/1 in overhang. Melt
the chocolate. Dissolve the cocoa in the
hot coffee to make a paste. Set aside.
2 Using a hand-held mixer, beat the egg
yolks with half the sugar in a mixing bowl
until pale and thick. Slowly beat in the
melted chocolate and cocoa-coffee paste
until just blended. In a separate bowl,
beat the egg whites and cream of tartar
until stiff peaks form. Sprinkle the
remaining sugar over the whites in two
batches and beat until the whites are
stiff and glossy, then beat in the
vanilla essence.
3 Stir a spoonful of the whites into the
chocolate mixture to lighten it, then
fold in the rest. Spoon into the tin.
Bake for 20–25 minutes or until the
cake springs back when touched with
a fingertip.

4 Dust a dish towel with cocoa. Turn the
cake out on to the towel immediately and
remove the paper. Trim off any crisp
edges. Starting at a narrow end, roll the
cake and towel together Swiss roll
fashion. Cool completely.

5 Make the filling. Whip the cream and
rum or liqueur until soft peaks form.
Beat a spoonful of cream into the
chestnut purée to lighten it, then fold in
the remaining cream and grated
chocolate. Set aside a quarter of this
mixture for the decoration. Unroll the
cake and spread chestnut cream to within
2.5 cm/1 in of the edge.
6 Using a dish towel to lift the cake,
carefully roll it up again. Place seam-
side down on a serving plate. Spread
some of the reserved chestnut cream
over the top and use the rest for
piped rosettes. Decorate with the
glacé chestnuts.

MARBLED SWISS ROLL

SERVES 6–8

90g / 3½oz / scant 1 cup plain flour
15ml / 1 tbsp cocoa powder
25g / 1oz plain chocolate, grated
25g / 1oz white chocolate, grated
3 eggs
115g / 4oz / ½ cup caster sugar
30ml / 2 tbsp boiling water
FOR THE FILLING
1 quantity Chocolate Buttercream
45ml / 3 tbsp chopped walnuts

1 Preheat oven to 200°C/400°F/Gas 6. Grease a 30 x 20 cm / 12 x 8 in Swiss roll tin and line with non-stick baking paper. Sift half the flour with the cocoa into a bowl. Stir in the grated plain chocolate. Sift the remaining flour into another bowl. Stir in the grated white chocolate.

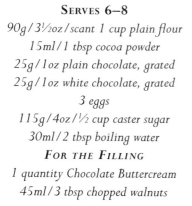

2 Whisk the eggs and sugar in a heatproof bowl set over a saucepan of hot water until it holds its shape when the whisk is lifted and a ribbon trail remains.
3 Remove the bowl from the heat and tip half the mixture into a separate bowl. Fold the plain chocolate mixture into one portion, then fold the white chocolate mixture into the other. Stir 15ml / 1 tbsp boiling water into each half to soften.

BAKED ALASKA
For a delicious dessert that takes only minutes to prepare, make individual Baked Alaskas by topping slices of the roll with chocolate ice cream, covering both cake and ice cream thickly with meringue mixture and baking at 230°C/450°F/Gas 8 for 2–3 minutes, watching carefully, until the meringue is tinged with brown.

4 Place alternate spoonfuls of mixture in the prepared tin and swirl lightly together with a knife or slim metal skewer for a marbled effect. Bake for about 12–15 minutes or until the cake is firm and the surface springs back when touched with a fingertip. Turn the cake out on to a sheet of non-stick baking paper placed flat on the work surface.

5 Trim the edges to neaten and cover with a damp, clean dish towel. Cool.
6 For the filling, mix the chocolate buttercream and walnuts in a bowl. Uncover the sponge, lift off the lining paper and spread the surface with the buttercream. Roll up carefully from a long side and place on a serving plate. Slice to serve, and store in an airtight container.

STICKY CHOCOLATE, MAPLE AND WALNUT SWIRLS

SERVES 12

450g / 1lb / 4 cups strong white flour
2.5m / ½ tsp ground cinnamon
50g / 2oz / ¼ cup unsalted butter, cut into
small pieces
50g / 2oz / ¼ cup caster sugar
1 sachet easy-blend dried yeast
1 egg yolk
120ml / 4fl oz / ½ cup water
60ml / 4 tbsp milk
45ml / 3 tbsp maple syrup, to finish

FOR THE FILLING

40g / 1½oz / 3 tbsp unsalted butter, melted
50g / 2oz / ⅓ cup light muscovado sugar
175g / 6oz / 1 cup plain chocolate chips
75g / 3oz / ¾ cup chopped walnuts

1 Grease a deep 23 cm / 9 in springform cake tin. Sift the flour and cinnamon into a bowl, then rub in the butter until the mixture resembles coarse breadcrumbs.

2 Stir in the sugar and yeast. In a jug or bowl, beat the egg yolk with the water and milk, then stir into the dry ingredients to make a soft dough.
3 Knead the dough on a lightly floured surface until smooth, then roll out to a rectangle measuring about 40 x 30 cm / 16 x 12 in.

4 For the filling, brush the dough with the melted butter and sprinkle with the sugar, chocolate chips and nuts.

5 Roll up the dough from one long side like a Swiss roll, then cut into 12 thick even-size slices. Pack close together in the tin, cut sides up. Cover and leave in a warm place for about 1½ hours, until well risen and springy. Meanwhile, preheat oven to 220°C/425°F/Gas 7.
6 Bake for 30–35 minutes, until golden brown. Remove from the tin and cool on a wire rack. Brush with maple syrup while still warm. Pull swirls apart to serve.

SPECIAL OCCASION CAKES

CHOCOLATE DATE TORTE

SERVES 8

4 egg whites
115g/4oz/½ cup caster sugar
200g/7oz plain chocolate
175g/6oz/scant 1 cup Medjool dates, pitted
and finely chopped
175g/6oz/1½ cups walnuts or pecan
nuts, chopped
5ml/1 tsp vanilla essence

FOR THE FROSTING

200g/7oz/scant 1 cup fromage frais
200g/7oz/scant 1 cup mascarpone
few drops of vanilla essence
icing sugar, to taste

1 Preheat oven to 180°C/350°F/Gas 4. Grease a round 20 cm/8 in springform cake tin. Line the base of the tin with non-stick baking paper.

2 Make the frosting. Mix together the fromage frais and mascarpone, add a few drops of vanilla essence and icing sugar to taste, then set aside.

3 Whisk the egg whites in a bowl until they form stiff peaks. Whisk in 30ml/ 2 tbsp of the caster sugar until the meringue is thick and glossy, then fold in the remainder.

4 Chop 175g/6 oz of the chocolate, then carefully fold into the meringue with the dates, nuts and vanilla essence. Pour into the prepared tin, spread level and bake for about 45 minutes, until risen around the edges.

5 Allow the cake to cool in the tin for 10 minutes, then invert on a wire rack. Peel off the lining paper and leave until completely cold.

6 Swirl the frosting over the top of the torte. Melt the remaining chocolate. Use a small paper piping bag to drizzle the chocolate over the torte. Work quickly and keep up an even pressure on the piping bag. Chill the torte before serving, then cut into wedges. This torte is best eaten on the day it is made.

QUEEN OF SHEBA CAKE

SERVES 8–10

*100g/3½oz/scant 1 cup whole blanched
almonds, lightly toasted
115g/4oz/½ cup caster sugar
40g/1½oz/⅓ cup plain flour
115g/4oz/½ cup unsalted butter, softened
150g/5oz plain chocolate, melted
3 eggs, separated
30ml/2 tbsp almond liqueur (optional)
chopped toasted almonds, to decorate*

FOR THE CHOCOLATE GLAZE

*175ml/6fl oz/¾ cup whipping cream
225g/8oz plain chocolate, chopped
25g/1oz/2 tbsp unsalted butter
30ml/2 tbsp almond liqueur (optional)*

1 Preheat oven to 180°C/350°F/Gas 4. Grease and base-line a 20–23 cm/8–9 in springform cake tin. Dust the tin lightly with flour.

2 In the bowl of a food processor fitted with a metal blade, process the almonds and 30ml/2 tbsp of the sugar until very fine. Transfer to a bowl and sift over the flour. Stir to mix, then set aside.

3 Beat the butter until creamy, then add half of the remaining sugar and beat for about 1–2 minutes until very light. Gradually beat in the melted chocolate, then add the egg yolks one at a time, beating well after each addition. Beat in the liqueur, if using.

4 In another bowl, beat the egg whites until soft peaks form. Add the remaining sugar and beat until the whites are stiff and glossy, but not dry. Fold a quarter of the whites into the chocolate mixture to lighten it, then alternately fold in the almond mixture and the remaining whites in three batches. Spoon the mixture into the prepared tin and spread evenly.

5 Bake for 30–35 minutes, until the edges are puffed but the centre is still soft. Cool in the tin for 15 minutes, then remove the sides and invert the cake on a wire rack. When quite cold, lift off the base of the tin and the paper.

6 To make the chocolate glaze, bring the cream to the boil in a saucepan. Remove from the heat and add the chocolate, stirring gently until it has melted and the mixture is smooth. Beat in the butter and almond liqueur, if using. Cool for about 20–30 minutes, until slightly thickened, stirring occasionally.

7 Place the cake on the wire rack over a baking sheet and pour over most of the warm glaze to cover completely. Cool slightly, then press the nuts on to the sides of the cake. Use the remaining glaze for a piped decoration. Transfer to a plate and chill until ready to serve.

SACHERTORTE

SERVES 10–12

225g/8oz plain dark chocolate, chopped into
small pieces
150g/5oz/⅔ cup butter, softened
115g/4oz/½ cup caster sugar
8 eggs, separated
115g/4oz/1 cup plain flour
FOR THE GLAZE
225g/8oz/scant 1 cup apricot jam
15ml/1 tbsp lemon juice
FOR THE ICING
225g/8oz plain dark chocolate, cut into
small pieces
200g/7oz/scant 1 cup caster sugar
15ml/1 tbsp golden syrup
250ml/8fl oz/1 cup double cream
5ml/1 tsp vanilla essence
plain chocolate leaves, to decorate

1 Preheat oven to 180°C/350°F/Gas 4. Grease a 23 cm/9 in round springform cake tin and line with non-stick baking paper. Melt the chocolate in a heatproof bowl over barely simmering water, then set the bowl aside.

2 Cream the butter with the sugar in a mixing bowl until pale and fluffy, then add the egg yolks, one at a time, beating after each addition. Beat in the melted chocolate, then sift the flour over the mixture and fold it in evenly.

3 Whisk the egg whites in a clean, grease-free bowl until stiff, then stir about a quarter of the whites into the chocolate mixture to lighten it. Fold in the remaining whites.

4 Tip the chocolate mixture into the prepared cake tin and smooth level. Bake for about 50–55 minutes or until firm. Cool in the tin for 5 minutes, then turn out carefully on to a wire rack and leave to cool completely.

5 Make the glaze. Heat the apricot jam with the lemon juice in a small saucepan until melted, then strain through a sieve into a bowl. Once the cake is cold, slice in half across the middle to make two even-size layers.

6 Brush the top and sides of each layer with the apricot glaze, then sandwich them together. Place on a wire rack.

7 Make the icing. Mix the chocolate, sugar, golden syrup, cream and vanilla essence in a heavy saucepan. Heat gently, stirring constantly, until the mixture is thick and smooth. Simmer gently for 3–5 minutes, without stirring, until the mixture registers 95°C/200°F on a sugar thermometer. Pour the icing quickly over the cake, spreading to cover the top and sides completely. Leave to set, decorate with chocolate leaves, then serve with whipped cream, if wished.

CHOCOLATE CHRISTMAS LOG

SERVES 12–14

*1 chocolate Swiss roll, see Chocolate
Chestnut Roulade*

*1 quantity of Chocolate Ganache or
Buttercream*

**FOR THE WHITE CHOCOLATE
CREAM FILLING**

*200g/7oz fine quality white chocolate,
chopped into small pieces*

475ml/16fl oz/2 cups double cream

*30ml/2 tbsp brandy or chocolate-flavoured
liqueur (optional)*

FOR THE CRANBERRY SAUCE

*450g/1lb fresh or frozen cranberries, rinsed
and picked over*

*275g/10oz/1 cup seedless raspberry
preserve, melted*

*115g/4oz/½ cup granulated sugar, or
to taste*

1 Make the cranberry sauce. Process the
cranberries in a food processor fitted with
a metal blade, until liquid. Press through
a sieve into a small bowl, and discard
pulp. Stir in the melted raspberry
preserve and the sugar to taste. If the
sauce is too thick, add a little water to
thin. Cover and place in the fridge.

2 Make the filling. In a small pan, heat the
chocolate with 120ml/4 fl oz/½ cup of
the cream until melted, stirring. Strain
into a bowl and cool to room
temperature. In a separate bowl, beat the
remaining cream with the brandy or
liqueur until soft peaks form; fold into
the chocolate mixture.

3 Unroll the Swiss roll, spread with the
mixture and roll up again from a long
end. Cut off a quarter of the roll at an
angle and arrange both pieces on a cake
board to resemble a log.

4 If using chocolate ganache for the
topping, allow it to soften to room
temperature, then beat to a soft,
spreading consistency. Cover the log with
ganache or buttercream and mark it with
a fork to resemble bark. Dust lightly with
icing sugar and top with a sprig of holly
or similar Christmas decoration. Serve
with the cranberry sauce.

MERINGUE MUSHROOMS

Small, decorative mushrooms are
traditionally used to decorate the
yule log. Using meringue mix, pipe
the "caps" and "stems" separately, dry
out in a low oven, then sandwich
together with ganache or chocolate
buttercream. Dust with cocoa, if you
like. Alternatively, shape mushrooms
from marzipan.

RICH CHOCOLATE LEAF GATEAU

SERVES 8

75g / 3oz plain dark chocolate, broken into squares
150ml / ¼ pint / ⅔ cup milk
175g / 6oz / ¾ cup unsalted butter, softened
250g / 9oz / 1⅓ cups light muscovado sugar
3 eggs
250g / 9oz / 2¼ cups plain flour
10ml / 2 tsp baking powder
75ml / 5 tbsp single cream

FOR THE FILLING AND TOPPING

60ml / 4 tbsp raspberry conserve
1 quantity Chocolate Ganache
dark and white chocolate leaves

<u>1</u> Preheat oven to 190°C / 375°F / Gas 5. Grease and base-line two 22 cm / 8½ in sandwich cake tins. Melt the chocolate with the milk over a low heat and allow to cool slightly.

<u>2</u> Cream the butter with the light muscovado sugar in a mixing bowl until light and fluffy. Add the eggs, one at a time, beating well after each addition.

<u>3</u> Sift the flour and baking powder over the mixture and fold in gently but thoroughly. Stir in the chocolate mixture and the cream, mixing until smooth. Divide between the prepared tins and level the tops.

<u>4</u> Bake the cakes for 30–35 minutes or until they are well risen and firm to the touch. Cool in the tins for a few minutes, then turn out on to wire racks.

<u>5</u> Sandwich the cake layers together with the raspberry conserve. Spread the chocolate ganache over the cake and swirl with a knife. Place the cake on a serving plate, then decorate with the chocolate leaves.

CHOCOLATE BOX WITH CARAMEL MOUSSE AND BERRIES

SERVES 8–10

275g/10oz plain chocolate, chopped into
small pieces

FOR THE CARAMEL MOUSSE

4 x 50g/2oz chocolate-coated caramel bars,
coarsely chopped
25ml/1½ tbsp milk or water
350ml/12fl oz/1½ cups double cream
1 egg white

FOR THE CARAMEL SHARDS

115g/4oz/½ cup granulated sugar
60ml/4 tbsp water

FOR THE TOPPING

115g/4oz fine quality white chocolate,
chopped into small pieces
350ml/12fl oz/1½ cups double cream
450g/1lb mixed berries or cut up fruits such
as raspberries, strawberries, blackberries or
sliced nectarine and orange segments

<u>1</u> Prepare the chocolate box. Turn a 23 cm/9 in square baking tin bottom-side up. Mould a piece of foil around the tin, then turn it right side up and line it with the foil, pressing against the edges to make the foil as smooth as possible.

<u>2</u> Place the plain chocolate in a heatproof bowl over a saucepan of simmering water. Stir until the chocolate has melted and is smooth. Immediately pour the melted chocolate into the lined tin. Tilt to coat the bottom and sides evenly, keeping the top edges of the sides as straight as possible. As the chocolate coats the sides, tilt the pan again to coat the corners and sides once more. Chill until firm.

<u>3</u> Place the caramel bars and milk or water in a heatproof bowl. Place over a pan of simmering water and stir until melted. Remove the bowl from the heat and cool for 10 minutes, stirring occasionally.

<u>4</u> Using a hand-held electric mixer, whip the cream in a bowl until soft peaks form. Stir a spoonful of the whipped cream into the caramel mixture to lighten it, then fold in the remaining cream. In another bowl beat the egg white until just stiff. Fold the egg white into the mousse mixture. Pour into the box. Chill for several hours or overnight, until set.

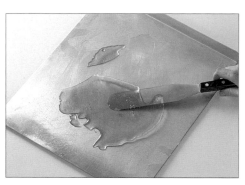

<u>5</u> Meanwhile, make the caramel shards. Lightly oil a baking sheet. In a small pan over a low heat, dissolve the sugar in the water, swirling the pan gently. Increase the heat and boil the mixture for 4–5 minutes, until the sugar begins to turn a pale golden colour. Protecting your hand with an oven glove, immediately pour the mixture on to the oiled sheet. Tilt the sheet to distribute the caramel in an even layer. (*Do not touch – caramel is dangerously hot.*) Cool completely, then using a metal palette knife, lift the caramel off the baking sheet and break into pieces.

<u>6</u> Make the topping. Combine the white chocolate and 120ml/4fl oz/½ cup of the cream in a small pan and melt over a low heat until smooth, stirring frequently. Strain into a medium bowl and cool to room temperature, stirring occasionally. In another bowl, beat the remaining cream with a hand-held electric mixer, until firm peaks form. Stir a spoonful of cream into the white chocolate mixture, then gently fold in the remaining whipped cream.

<u>7</u> Using the foil as a guide, remove the mousse-filled box from the tin and peel the foil carefully from the sides, then the bottom. Slide the box gently on to a serving plate.

<u>8</u> Spoon the chocolate-cream mixture into a piping bag fitted with a medium star tip. Pipe a decorative design of rosettes or shells over the surface of the set mousse. Decorate the cream-topped box with the mixed berries or cut up fruits and the caramel shards.

DOUBLE HEART ENGAGEMENT CAKE

SERVES 20
*double quantity One-Mix Chocolate
Sponge mixture
double quantity Chocolate Buttercream
icing sugar, for sifting
chocolate curls and fresh raspberries,
to decorate*

VARIATIONS

Use plain buttercream, tinted to a
delicate shade of rose. Decorate with
strawberries, half-dipped in melted
chocolate.
Cover the cakes with Chocolate
Ganache and drizzle melted
chocolate over the top. Arrange
chocolate-dipped fruit on top.
Cover both the cakes with Chocolate
Fondant and top with pale apricot or
cream sugar roses and chocolate
leaves. Trim each cake with a narrow
apricot or cream ribbon.

1 Preheat oven to 160°C/325°F/Gas 3.
Grease and base-line with greaseproof
paper two 20 cm/8 in heart-shaped cake
tins. Divide the one-mix chocolate
sponge cake mixture evenly between the
tins and smooth the surfaces. Bake for 30
minutes. Turn on to a wire rack, peel off
the lining paper and leave to cool.

2 Cut each cake in half horizontally. Use
about one-third of the buttercream to fill
both cakes, then sandwich them together
to make two. Cover the tops of the cakes
with buttercream.

3 Arrange on a cake board. Use the
remaining icing to coat the sides of the
cakes. Make sure it is thickly covered.

4 Generously cover the tops and sides
of both the cakes with the chocolate
curls, beginning from the top of the heart
and arranging them as shown, and
pressing them gently into the
buttercream as you go.
5 Dust a little icing sugar over the top of
each cake and decorate with raspberries.
Chill until ready to serve.

Black Forest Gateau

4 Prick each layer all over with a skewer or fork, then sprinkle with Kirsch. Using a hand-held electric mixer, whip the cream in a bowl until it starts to thicken, then gradually beat in the icing sugar and vanilla essence until the mixture begins to hold its shape.

5 To assemble, spread one cake layer with a thick layer of flavoured cream and top with about half the cherries. Spread a second cake layer with cream, top with the remaining cherries, then place it on top of the first layer. Top with the final cake layer.

6 Spread the remaining cream all over the cake. Dust a plate with icing sugar, and position the cake carefully in the centre. Press grated chocolate over the sides and decorate the cake with the chocolate curls and fresh or drained cherries.

Serves 8–10
6 eggs
200g / 7oz / scant 1 cup caster sugar
5ml / 1 tsp vanilla essence
50g / 2oz / ½ cup plain flour
50g / 2oz / ½ cup cocoa powder
115g / 4oz / ½ cup unsalted butter, melted

For the Filling and Topping
60ml / 4 tbsp Kirsch
600ml / 1 pint / 2½ cups double cream
30ml / 2 tbsp icing sugar
2.5ml / ½ tsp vanilla essence
675g / 1½lb jar stoned morello cherries, well drained

To Decorate
icing sugar, for dusting
grated chocolate
Chocolate Curls
fresh or drained canned morello cherries

1 Preheat oven to 180°C/350°F/Gas 4. Grease three 19 cm/7½ in sandwich cake tins. Line the bottom of each with non-stick baking paper. Combine the eggs with the sugar and vanilla essence in a bowl and beat with a hand-held electric mixer until pale and very thick.

2 Sift the flour and cocoa powder over the mixture and fold in lightly and evenly with a metal spoon. Gently stir in the melted butter.

3 Divide the mixture among the prepared cake tins, smoothing them level. Bake for 15–18 minutes, until the cakes have risen and are springy to the touch. Leave them to cool in the tins for about 5 minutes, then turn out on to wire racks and leave to cool completely. Remove the lining paper from each cake layer.

WHITE CHOCOLATE CAPPUCCINO GATEAU

SERVES 8

4 eggs
115g/4oz/½ cup caster sugar
15ml/1 tbsp strong black coffee
2.5ml/½ tsp vanilla essence
115g/4oz/1 cup plain flour
75g/3oz white chocolate, coarsely grated
FOR THE FILLING
120ml/4fl oz/½ cup double cream or
whipping cream
15ml/1 tbsp coffee liqueur
FOR THE FROSTING AND TOPPING
15ml/1 tbsp coffee liqueur
1 quantity White Chocolate Frosting
white chocolate curls
cocoa powder or ground cinnamon,
for dusting

<u>1</u> Preheat oven to 180°C/350°F/Gas 4. Grease two 18 cm/7 in round sandwich cake tins and line the base of each with non-stick baking paper.

<u>2</u> Combine the eggs, caster sugar, coffee and vanilla essence in a large heatproof bowl. Place over a saucepan of hot water and whisk until pale and thick.

<u>3</u> Sift half the flour over the mixture; fold in gently and evenly. Fold in the remaining flour with the grated white chocolate.

<u>4</u> Divide the mixture between the prepared tins and smooth level. Bake for 20–25 minutes, until firm and golden brown, then turn out on wire racks and leave to cool completely.

<u>5</u> Make the filling. Whip the cream with the coffee liqueur in a bowl until it holds its shape. Spread over one of the cakes, then place the second layer on top.

<u>6</u> Stir the coffee liqueur into the frosting. Spread over the top and sides of the cake, swirling with a palette knife. Top with curls of white chocolate and dust with cocoa or cinnamon. Transfer the cake to a serving plate and set aside until the frosting has set. Serve the gâteau on the day it was made, if possible.

CHOCOLATE BRANDY SNAP GATEAU

SERVES 8

225g/8oz plain dark chocolate, chopped
225g/8oz/1 cup unsalted butter, softened
200g/7oz/generous 1 cup dark
muscovado sugar
6 eggs, separated
5ml/1 tsp vanilla essence
150g/5oz/1¼ cups ground hazelnuts
60ml/4 tbsp fresh white breadcrumbs
finely grated rind of 1 large orange
1 quantity Chocolate Ganache, for filling
and frosting
icing sugar, for dusting

FOR THE BRANDY SNAPS

50g/2oz/¼ cup unsalted butter
50g/2oz/¼ cup caster sugar
75g/3oz/⅓ cup golden syrup
50g/2oz/½ cup plain flour
5ml/1 tsp brandy

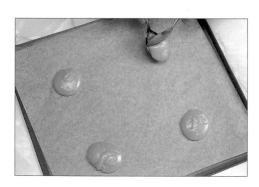

1 Preheat oven to 180°C/350°F/Gas 4. Grease two 20 cm/8 in sandwich cake tins and line the base of each with non-stick baking paper. Melt the chocolate and set aside to cool slightly.

2 Cream the butter with the sugar in a mixing bowl until pale and fluffy. Beat in the egg yolks and vanilla essence. Add the chocolate and mix thoroughly.

3 In a clean, grease-free bowl, whisk the egg whites to soft peaks, then fold them into the chocolate mixture with the ground hazelnuts, breadcrumbs and orange rind.

4 Divide the cake mixture between the prepared tins and smooth the tops. Bake for 25–30 minutes or until well risen and firm. Turn out on to wire racks. Leave the oven on.

5 Make the brandy snaps. Line two baking sheets with non-stick baking paper. Melt the butter, sugar and syrup together.

6 Stir the butter mixture until smooth. Remove from the heat and stir in the flour and brandy.

7 Place small spoonfuls of the mixture well apart on the baking sheets and bake for 8–10 minutes, until golden. Cool for a few seconds until firm enough to lift on to a wire rack.

8 Immediately pinch the edges of each brandy snap to create a frilled effect. If the biscuits become too firm, soften them briefly in the oven.

9 Sandwich the cake layers together with half the chocolate ganache, transfer to a plate and spread the remaining ganache on the top. Arrange the brandy snaps over the gâteau and dust with icing sugar.

COOK'S TIP

To save time, you could use ready-made brandy snaps. Simply warm them for a few minutes in the oven until they are pliable enough to shape. Or use as they are, filling them with cream, and arranging them so that they fan out from the centre of the gâteau.

CHOCOLATE ALMOND MOUSSE CAKE

SERVES 8

*50g/2oz plain dark chocolate, broken
into squares*
200g/7oz marzipan, grated or chopped
200ml/7fl oz/scant 1 cup milk
115g/4oz/1 cup self-raising flour
2 eggs, separated
*75g/3oz/½ cup light muscovado
sugar*

FOR THE MOUSSE FILLING

*115g/4oz plain chocolate, chopped into
small pieces*
50g/2oz/¼ cup unsalted butter
2 eggs, separated
*30ml/2 tbsp Amaretto di Saronno
liqueur*

FOR THE TOPPING

1 quantity Chocolate Ganache
toasted flaked almonds, to decorate

1 Preheat oven to 190°C/375°F/Gas 5. Grease a deep 17 cm/6½ in square cake tin and line with non-stick baking paper. Combine the chocolate, marzipan and milk in a saucepan and heat gently without boiling, stirring until smooth.

2 Sift the flour into a bowl and add the chocolate mixture and egg yolks, beating until evenly mixed.

3 Whisk the egg whites in a clean, grease-free bowl until stiff enough to hold firm peaks. Whisk in the sugar gradually. Stir about 15ml/1 tbsp of the whites into the chocolate mixture to lighten it, then fold in the rest.

4 Spoon the mixture into the tin, spreading it evenly. Bake for 45–50 minutes, until well risen, firm and springy to the touch. Leave to cool on a wire rack.

5 Make the mousse filling. Melt the chocolate with the butter in a small saucepan over a low heat, then remove from the heat and beat in the egg yolks and Amaretto. Whisk the egg whites in a clean, grease-free bowl until stiff, then fold into the chocolate mixture.

6 Slice the cold cake in half across the middle to make two even layers. Return one half to the clean cake tin and pour over the chocolate mousse. Top with the second layer of cake and press down lightly. Chill until set.

7 Turn the cake out on to a serving plate. Allow the chocolate ganache to soften to room temperature, then beat it to a soft, spreading consistency. Spread the chocolate ganache over the top and sides of the cake, then press toasted flaked almonds over the sides. Serve chilled.

CHOCOLATE GINGER CRUNCH CAKE

SERVES 6

150g/5oz plain chocolate, chopped into small pieces
50g/2oz/¼ cup unsalted butter
115g/4oz ginger nut biscuits
4 pieces of preserved stem ginger
30ml/2 tbsp stem ginger syrup
45ml/3 tbsp desiccated coconut

TO DECORATE

25g/1oz milk chocolate, chopped into small pieces
pieces of crystallized ginger

1 Grease a 15 cm/6 in flan ring and place it on a sheet of non-stick baking paper. Melt the plain chocolate with the butter in a heatproof bowl over barely simmering water. Remove from the heat and set aside.

2 Crush the biscuits into small pieces. Tip them into a bowl.

3 Chop the stem ginger fairly finely and mix with the crushed ginger nut biscuits.

4 Stir the biscuit mixture, ginger syrup and coconut into the melted chocolate and butter, mixing well until evenly combined.

5 Tip the mixture into the prepared flan ring and press down firmly and evenly. Chill in the fridge until set.

6 Remove the flan ring and slide the cake on to a plate. Melt the milk chocolate, drizzle it over the top and decorate with the pieces of crystallized ginger.

FROSTED CHOCOLATE FUDGE CAKE

SERVES 6–8

115g/4oz plain chocolate, chopped into small pieces
175g/6oz/¾ cup unsalted butter or margarine, softened
200g/7oz/generous 1 cup light muscovado sugar
5ml/1 tsp vanilla essence
3 eggs, beaten
150ml/¼ pint/⅔ cup Greek-style yogurt
150g/5oz/1¼ cups self-raising flour
icing sugar and chocolate curls, to decorate

FOR THE FROSTING

115g/4 oz plain dark chocolate, chopped into small pieces
50g/2oz/¼ cup unsalted butter
350g/12oz/2¼ cups icing sugar
90ml/6 tbsp Greek-style yogurt

1 Preheat oven to 190°C/375°F/Gas 5. Lightly grease two 20 cm/8 in round sandwich cake tins and line the base of each with non-stick baking paper. Melt the chocolate.

2 In a mixing bowl, cream the butter or margarine with the sugar until light and fluffy. Beat in the vanilla essence, then gradually add the beaten eggs, beating well after each addition.

3 Stir in the melted plain chocolate and yogurt evenly. Fold in the flour with a metal spoon.

4 Divide the mixture between the prepared tins. Bake for 25–30 minutes or until the cakes are firm to the touch. Turn out and cool on a wire rack.

5 Make the frosting. Melt the chocolate and butter in a saucepan over a low heat. Remove from the heat and stir in the icing sugar and yogurt. Mix with a rubber spatula until smooth, then beat until the frosting begins to cool and thicken slightly. Use about a third of the mixture to sandwich the cakes together.

6 Working quickly, spread the remainder over the top and sides. Sprinkle with icing sugar and decorate with chocolate curls.

WHITE CHOCOLATE CELEBRATION CAKE

SERVES 40–50

900g / 2lb / 8 cups plain flour
2.5ml / ½ tsp salt
20ml / 4 tsp bicarbonate of soda
450g / 1lb white chocolate, chopped
475ml / 16fl oz / 2 cups whipping cream
450g / 1lb / 2 cups unsalted butter, softened
900g / 2lb / 4 cups caster sugar
12 eggs
20ml / 4 tsp lemon essence
grated rind of 2 lemons
335ml / 11fl oz / 1⅓ cups buttermilk
lemon curd, for filling
chocolate leaves, to decorate

FOR THE LEMON SYRUP
200g / 7oz / scant 1 cup granulated sugar
250ml / 8fl oz / 1 cup water
60ml / 4 tbsp lemon juice

FOR THE BUTTERCREAM
675g / 1½lb white chocolate chopped
1kg / 2¼lb cream cheese, softened
500g / 1¼lb / 2½ cups unsalted butter, at room temperature
60ml / 4 tbsp lemon juice
5ml / 1 tsp lemon essence

1 Divide all the ingredients into two equal batches, so that the quantities are more manageable. Use each batch to make one cake. Preheat oven to 180°C / 350°F / Gas 4. Grease a 30 cm / 12 in round cake tin. Base-line with non-stick baking paper. Sift the flour, salt and bicarbonate of soda into a bowl and set aside. Melt the chocolate and cream in a saucepan over a medium heat, stirring until smooth. Set aside to cool to room temperature.

VARIATION

For a summer celebration, decorate the cake with raspberries and white chocolate petals. To make the petals, you will need about 20 x 7.5 cm / 3 in foil squares. Spread melted white chocolate thinly over each piece of foil, so that it resembles a rose petal. Before the chocolate sets, bend the foil up to emphasize the petal shape. When set, peel away the foil.

2 Beat the butter until creamy, then add the sugar and beat for 2–3 minutes. Beat in the eggs, then slowly beat in the melted chocolate, lemon essence and rind. Gradually add the flour mixture, alternately with the buttermilk, to make a smooth pouring mixture. Pour into the tin and bake for 1 hour or until a skewer inserted in the cake comes out clean.

3 Cool in the tin for 10 minutes, then invert the cake on a wire rack and cool completely. Wrap in clear film until ready to assemble. Using the second batch of ingredients, make another cake in the same way.

4 Make the lemon syrup. In a small saucepan, combine the sugar and water. Over a medium heat, bring to the boil, stirring until the sugar dissolves. Remove from the heat, stir in the lemon juice and cool completely. Store in an airtight container until required.

5 Make the buttercream. Melt the chocolate. Cool slightly. Beat the cream cheese in a bowl until smooth. Gradually beat in the cooled white chocolate, then the butter, lemon juice and essence. Chill.

6 Split each cake in half. Spoon syrup over each layer, let it soak in, then repeat. Spread the bottom half of each cake with lemon curd and replace the tops.

7 Gently beat the buttercream in a bowl until creamy. Spread a quarter over the top of one of the filled cakes. Place the second filled cake on top. Spread a small amount of softened butter over the top and sides of the cake to create a smooth, crumb-free surface. Chill for 15 minutes, so that the buttercream sets a little.

8 Place the cake on a serving plate. Set aside a quarter of the remaining buttercream for piping, then spread the rest evenly over the top and sides of the filled cake.

9 Spoon the reserved buttercream into a large icing bag fitted with a small star tip. Pipe a shell pattern around the rim of the cake. Decorate with chocolate leaves, made with dark or white chocolate (or a mixture) and fresh flowers.

HOT DESSERTS

CHOCOLATE CINNAMON CAKE WITH BANANA SAUCE

6 Fold a dollop of whites into the chocolate mixture to lighten it. Fold in the remaining whites in three batches, alternating with the sifted flour mixture.

7 Pour the mixture into the prepared tin. Bake for 40-50 minutes or until a skewer inserted in the centre comes out clean. Turn the cake out on to a wire rack. Preheat the grill.

8 Make the sauce. Slice the bananas into a shallow, flameproof dish. Stir in the brown sugar and lemon juice. Place under the grill for 8 minutes, stirring occasionally, until caramelized.

9 Mash the banana mixture until almost smooth. Tip into a bowl and stir in the cream and rum, if using. Slice the cake and serve with the sauce.

SERVES 6

25g/1oz plain chocolate, chopped into small pieces
115g/4oz/½ cup unsalted butter, at room temperature
15ml/1 tbsp instant coffee powder
5 eggs, separated
225g/8oz/1 cup granulated sugar
115g/4oz/1 cup plain flour
10ml/2 tsp ground cinnamon

FOR THE SAUCE

4 ripe bananas
45ml/3 tbsp soft light brown sugar
15ml/8oz/1 tbsp fresh lemon juice
175ml/6fl oz/¾ cup whipping cream
15ml/1 tbsp rum (optional)

1 Preheat oven to 180°C/350°F/Gas 4. Grease a 20 cm/8 in round cake tin.

2 Combine the chocolate and butter in the top of a double boiler or in a heatproof bowl set over a saucepan of simmering water. Stir until melted. Remove from the heat and stir in the coffee. Set aside.

3 Beat the egg yolks with the granulated sugar until thick and lemon-coloured. Add the chocolate mixture and beat on low speed until just blended.

4 Stir the flour and cinnamon together in a bowl.

5 In another bowl, beat the egg whites until they hold stiff peaks.

STEAMED CHOCOLATE AND FRUIT PUDDINGS WITH CHOCOLATE SYRUP

SERVES 4

115g / 4oz / ⅔ cup dark muscovado sugar
1 eating apple
75g / 3oz / ¾ cup cranberries, thawed if frozen
115g / 4oz / ½ cup soft margarine
2 eggs
115g / 4oz / ½ cup self-raising flour
45ml / 3 tbsp cocoa powder

FOR THE CHOCOLATE SYRUP

115g / 4oz plain chocolate, chopped
30ml / 2 tbsp clear honey
15ml / ½oz / 1 tbsp unsalted butter
2.5ml / ½ tsp vanilla essence

1 Prepare a steamer or half fill a saucepan with water and bring it to the boil. Grease four individual pudding basins and sprinkle each one with a little of the muscovado sugar to coat well all over.
2 Peel and core the apple. Dice it into a bowl, add the cranberries and mix well. Divide the fruit among the prepared pudding basins.
3 Place the remaining muscovado sugar in a mixing bowl. Add the margarine, eggs, flour and cocoa. Beat until combined and smooth.

4 Spoon the mixture into the basins and cover each with a double thickness of foil. Steam for about 45 minutes, topping up the boiling water as required, until the puddings are well risen and firm.
5 Make the syrup. Mix the chocolate, honey, butter and vanilla essence in a small saucepan. Heat gently, stirring until melted and smooth.
6 Run a knife around the edge of each pudding to loosen it, then turn out on to individual plates. Serve at once, with the chocolate syrup.

Rich Chocolate and Coffee Pudding

Serves 6

75g/3oz/¾ cup plain flour
10ml/2 tsp baking powder
pinch of salt
50g/2oz/¼ cup butter or margarine
25g/1oz plain chocolate, chopped into
small pieces
115g/4oz/½ cup caster sugar
75ml/3fl oz/5 tbsp milk
1.5ml/¼ tsp vanilla essence
whipped cream, for serving

For the Topping

30ml/2 tbsp instant coffee powder
325ml/11fl oz/generous ½ pint hot water
90g/3½oz/7 tbsp soft dark brown sugar
65g/2½oz/5 tbsp caster sugar
30ml/2 tbsp unsweetened cocoa powder

1 Preheat oven to 180°C/350°F/Gas 4. Grease a 23 cm/9 in square non-stick baking tin.

2 Sift the flour, baking powder and salt into a small bowl. Set aside.

3 Melt the butter or margarine, chocolate and caster sugar in a heatproof bowl set over a saucepan of simmering water, or in a double boiler, stirring occasionally. Remove the bowl from the heat.

4 Add the flour mixture and stir well. Stir in the milk and vanilla essence. Mix with a wooden spoon, then pour the mixture into the prepared baking tin.

5 Make the topping. Dissolve the coffee in the water in a bowl. Allow to cool.

6 Mix the brown sugar, caster sugar and cocoa powder in a bowl. Sprinkle the mixture over the pudding mixture.

7 Pour the coffee evenly over the surface. Bake for 40 minutes or until the pudding is risen and set on top. The coffee mixture will have formed a delicious creamy sauce underneath. Serve immediately with whipped cream.

DARK CHOCOLATE RAVIOLI WITH WHITE CHOCOLATE AND CREAM CHEESE FILLING

SERVES 4

175g / 6oz / 1½ cups plain flour
25g / 1oz / ¼ cup cocoa powder
salt
30ml / 2 tbsp icing sugar
2 large eggs, beaten
15ml / 1 tbsp olive oil
single cream and grated chocolate, to serve
FOR THE FILLING
175g / 6oz white chocolate, chopped
350g / 12oz / 3 cups cream cheese
1 egg, plus 1 beaten egg to seal

1 Make the pasta. Sift the flour with the cocoa, salt and icing sugar on to a work surface. Make a well in the centre and pour the eggs and oil in. Mix together with your fingers. Knead until smooth. Alternatively, make the dough in a food processor, then knead by hand. Cover and rest for at least 30 minutes.

2 To make the filling, melt the white chocolate in a heatproof bowl placed over a pan of simmering water. Cool slightly. Beat the cream cheese in a bowl, then beat in the chocolate and eggs. Spoon into a piping bag fitted with a plain nozzle.

3 Cut the dough in half and wrap one portion in clear film. Roll the pasta out thinly to a rectangle on a lightly floured surface, or use a pasta machine. Cover with a clean damp dish towel and repeat with the remaining pasta.

4 Pipe small mounds (about 5ml / 1 tsp) of filling in even rows, spacing them at 4 cm / 1½ in intervals across one piece of the dough. Using a pastry brush, brush the spaces of dough between the mounds with beaten egg.

5 Using a rolling pin, lift the remaining sheet of pasta over the dough with the filling. Press down firmly between the pockets of filling, pushing out any trapped air. Cut the filled chocolate pasta into rounds with a serrated ravioli cutter or sharp knife. Transfer to a floured dish towel. Leave for 1 hour to dry out, ready for cooking.

6 Bring a frying pan of water to the boil and add the ravioli a few at a time, stirring to prevent them sticking together. (Adding a few drops of a bland oil to the water will help, too.) Simmer gently for 3–5 minutes, remove with a perforated spoon and serve with a generous splash of single cream and grated chocolate.

Chocolate, Date and Walnut Pudding

Serves 4

25g/1oz/¼ cup chopped walnuts
25g/1oz/2 tbsp chopped dates
2 eggs
5ml/1 tsp vanilla essence
30ml/2 tbsp golden caster sugar
45ml/3 tbsp plain wholemeal flour
15ml/1 tbsp cocoa powder
30ml/2 tbsp skimmed milk

1 Preheat oven to 180°C/350°F/Gas 4. Grease and base-line with greaseproof paper a 1.2 litre/2 pint/5 cup pudding basin. Spoon in the walnuts and dates.

2 Combine the egg yolks, vanilla essence and sugar in a heatproof bowl. Place over a pan of hot water.

3 Whisk the egg whites to soft peaks. Whisk the egg yolk mixture until it is thick and pale, then remove the bowl from the heat. Sift the flour and cocoa over the mixture and fold them in with a metal spoon. Stir in the milk, to soften the mixture, then fold in the egg whites.

4 Spoon the mixture over the walnuts and dates in the basin and bake for 40–45 minutes or until the pudding is well risen and firm to the touch. Run a knife around the pudding to loosen it from the basin, and then turn it out on to a plate and serve immediately.

MAGIC CHOCOLATE MUD PUDDING

SERVES 4

50g / 2oz / 4 tbsp butter, plus extra for greasing
90g / 3½oz / scant 1 cup self-raising flour
5ml / 1 tsp ground cinnamon
75ml / 5 tbsp cocoa powder
200g / 7oz / generous 1 cup light muscovado or
demerara sugar
475ml / 16fl oz / 2 cups milk
crème fraîche, Greek-style yogurt or vanilla
ice cream, to serve

1 Preheat oven to 180°C/350°F/Gas 4. Prepare the dish: use the extra butter to grease a 1.5 litre/2½ pint/6¼ cup ovenproof dish. Place the dish on a baking sheet and set aside.

2 Sift the flour and ground cinnamon into a bowl. Sift in 15ml/1 tbsp of the cocoa and mix well.

3 Place the butter in a saucepan. Add 115g/4oz/½ cup of the sugar and 150ml/¼ pint/⅔ cup of the milk. Heat gently without boiling, stirring from time to time, until the butter has melted and all the sugar has dissolved. Remove the pan from the heat.

4 Stir in the flour mixture, mixing evenly. Pour the mixture into the prepared dish and level the surface.

5 Mix the remaining sugar and cocoa in a bowl, then sprinkle over the pudding mixture.

6 Pour the remaining milk evenly over the pudding.

7 Bake for 45–50 minutes or until the sponge has risen to the top and is firm to the touch. Serve hot, with the crème fraîche, yogurt or ice cream.

CHOCOLATE SOUFFLE CREPES

MAKES 12 CREPES

75g/3oz/¾ cup plain flour
15ml/1 tbsp cocoa powder
5ml/1 tsp caster sugar
pinch of salt
5ml/1 tsp ground cinnamon
2 eggs
175ml/6fl oz/¾ cup milk
5ml/1 tsp vanilla essence
50g/2oz/4 tbsp unsalted butter,
melted
raspberries, pineapple and mint sprigs,
to decorate

FOR THE PINEAPPLE SYRUP

½ medium pineapple, peeled, cored and
finely chopped
120ml/4fl oz/½ cup water
30ml/2 tbsp natural maple syrup
5ml/1 tsp cornflour
½ cinnamon stick
30ml/2 tbsp rum

FOR THE SOUFFLE FILLING

250g/9oz bittersweet chocolate, chopped into
small pieces
75ml/3fl oz/⅓ cup double cream
3 eggs, separated
25g/1oz/2 tbsp caster sugar

<u>1</u> Prepare the syrup. In a saucepan over a medium heat, bring the pineapple, water, maple syrup, cornflour and cinnamon stick to the boil. Simmer for 2–3 minutes, until the sauce thickens, whisking frequently. Remove from the heat and discard the cinnamon. Pour into a bowl, and stir in the rum. Cool, then chill.

COOK'S TIP
You might be able to find ready-made crêpes in the shops, which will save time.

<u>2</u> Prepare the crêpes. Sift the flour, cocoa, sugar, salt and cinnamon into a bowl. Stir, then make a well in the centre. In a bowl, beat the eggs, milk and vanilla. Gradually add to the well in the flour mixture, whisking in flour from the side of the bowl to form a smooth batter. Stir in half the melted butter and pour into a jug. Allow to stand for 1 hour.

<u>3</u> Heat an 18–20 cm/7–8 in crêpe pan. Brush with butter. Stir the batter. Pour 45ml/3 tbsp batter into the pan; swirl the pan to cover the bottom. Cook over a medium-high heat for 1–2 minutes until the bottom is golden. Turn over and cook for 30–45 seconds, then turn on to a plate. Stack between sheets of non-stick baking paper and set aside.

<u>4</u> Prepare the filling. In a saucepan over a medium heat, melt the chocolate and cream until smooth, stirring frequently.

<u>5</u> In a bowl, with a hand-held electric mixer, beat the yolks with half the sugar for 3–5 minutes, until light and creamy. Gradually beat in the chocolate mixture. Allow to cool. In a separate bowl with cleaned beaters, beat the egg whites until soft peaks form. Gradually beat in the remaining sugar until stiff peaks form. Beat a large spoonful of whites in to the chocolate mixture to lighten it, then fold in the remaining whites.

<u>6</u> Preheat oven to 200°C/400°F/Gas 6. Lay a crêpe on a plate, bottom side up. Spoon a little soufflé mixture on to the crêpe, spreading it to the edge. Fold the bottom half over the soufflé mixture, then fold in half again to form a filled triangle. Place on a buttered baking sheet. Repeat with the remaining crêpes. Brush the tops with melted butter and bake for 15–20 minutes, until the filling has souffléd. Decorate with raspberries, pineapple pieces and mint and serve with the syrup.

VARIATION
For a simpler version of the crêpes, just serve with a spoonful of maple syrup rather than making the pineapple syrup.

CHOCOLATE CHIP AND BANANA PUDDING

SERVES 4

200g/7oz/1¾ cups self-raising flour
75g/3oz/6 tbsp unsalted butter or margarine
2 ripe bananas
75g/3oz/6 tbsp caster sugar
60ml/4 tbsp milk
1 egg, beaten
60ml/4 tbsp plain chocolate chips or chopped chocolate
Glossy Chocolate Sauce, to serve

1 Prepare a steamer or half fill a saucepan with water and bring it to the boil. Grease a 1 litre/1¾ pint/4 cup pudding basin. Sift the flour into a bowl and rub in the unsalted butter or margarine until the mixture resembles coarse breadcrumbs.

2 Mash the bananas in a bowl. Stir them into the flour and butter mixture, then add the caster sugar and mix well.
3 Whisk the milk with the egg in a jug or small bowl, then beat into the pudding mixture. Stir in the chocolate chips or chopped chocolate.

4 Spoon the mixture into the prepared basin, cover closely with a double thickness of foil, and steam for 2 hours, topping up the water as required.
5 Run a knife around the top of the pudding to loosen it, then turn it out on to a serving dish. Serve hot, with the sauce.

CHOCOLATE, DATE AND ALMOND FILO COIL

SERVES 6

275g/10oz pack filo pastry, thawed if frozen
50g/2oz/4 tbsp unsalted butter, melted
icing sugar, cocoa powder and ground
cinnamon, for dusting

FOR THE FILLING

75g/3oz/6 tbsp unsalted butter
115g/4oz plain dark chocolate, chopped into
small pieces
115g/4oz/1 cup ground almonds
115g/4oz/⅔ cup chopped dates
75g/3oz/½ cup icing sugar
10ml/2 tsp rosewater
2.5ml/½ tsp ground cinnamon

1 Preheat oven to 180°C/350°F/Gas 4.
Grease a 22 cm/8½ in round cake tin.
Make the filling. Melt the butter with the
chocolate, then stir in the other ingredients
to make a paste. Leave to cool.

2 Lay one sheet of filo on a clean work
surface. Brush it lightly with melted
butter, then lay a second sheet on top and
brush that with melted butter too.

3 Roll a handful of the chocolate almond
mixture into a long sausage shape and
place along one long edge of the layered
filo. Roll the pastry tightly around the
filling to make a roll. Keep the roll even,
shaping it with your hands.

4 Place the roll in the tin, coiling it
around against the sides. Make enough
rolls to fill the tin and fit them in place.

5 Brush the coil with the remaining
melted butter. Bake in the oven for
30–35 minutes, until the pastry is golden
brown and crisp.

6 Remove the coil from the tin, and place
it on a plate. Serve warm, dusted with
icing sugar, cocoa and cinnamon.

Chocolate Almond Meringue Pie

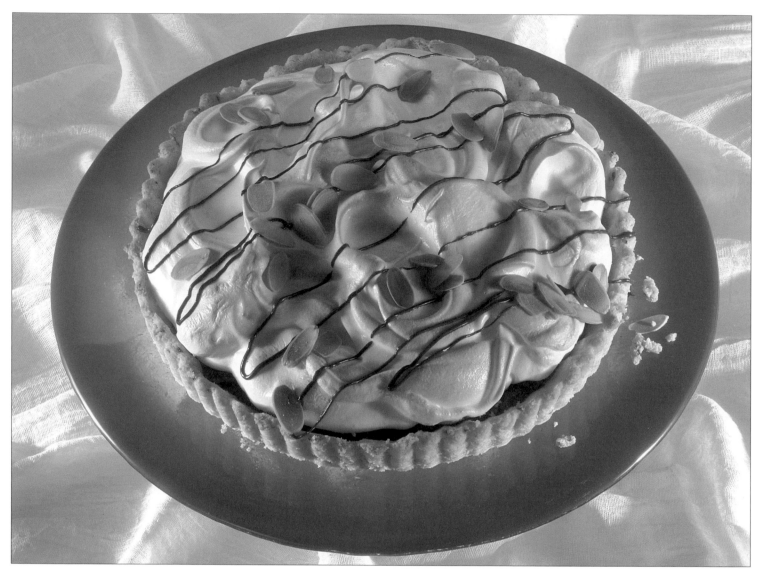

Serves 6

175g / 6oz / 1½ cups plain flour
50g / 2oz / ½ cup ground rice
150g / 5oz / ⅔ cup unsalted butter
finely grated rind of 1 orange
1 egg yolk
flaked almonds and melted plain dark
chocolate, to decorate

For the Filling

150g / 5oz plain dark chocolate, chopped into
small pieces
50g / 2oz / 4 tbsp unsalted butter, softened
75g / 3oz / 6 tbsp caster sugar
10ml / 2 tsp cornflour
4 egg yolks
75g / 3oz / ¾ cup ground almonds

For the Meringue

3 egg whites
150g / 5oz / ⅔ cup caster sugar

<u>1</u> Sift the flour and ground rice into a bowl. Rub in the butter until the mixture resembles breadcrumbs. Stir in the orange rind. Add the egg yolks; bring the dough together. Roll out and use to line a 23 cm / 9 in round flan tin. Chill.

<u>2</u> Preheat oven to 190°C / 375°F / Gas 5. Prick the pastry base, cover with grease-proof paper weighed down with baking beans and bake blind for 10 minutes.

<u>3</u> Make the filling. Melt the chocolate, then cream the butter with the sugar in a bowl, and beat in the cornflour and egg yolks. Fold in the almonds, then the melted chocolate. Remove the paper and beans from the pastry case and add the filling. Bake for a further 10 minutes.
<u>4</u> Make the meringue. Whisk the egg whites in a clean, grease-free bowl until stiff, then gradually whisk in about half the caster sugar. Fold in the remaining sugar with a metal spoon.
<u>5</u> Spoon the meringue over the chocolate filling, lifting it up with the back of the spoon to form peaks. Reduce the oven temperature to 180°C / 350°F / Gas 4 and bake the pie for 15–20 minutes or until the topping is pale gold. Serve warm, scattered with the almonds and drizzled with the melted chocolate.

CHOCOLATE PECAN PIE

SERVES 6

200g / 7oz / 1¾ cups plain flour
75ml / 5 tbsp caster sugar
90g / 3½oz / scant ½ cup unsalted butter,
softened
1 egg, beaten
finely grated rind of 1 orange

FOR THE FILLING

200g / 7oz / ¾ cup golden syrup
45ml / 3 tbsp soft light muscovado sugar
150g / 5oz plain chocolate, chopped into
small pieces
50g / 2oz / ¼ cup butter
3 eggs, beaten
5ml / 1 tsp vanilla essence
175g / 6oz / 1½ cups pecan nuts

1 Sift the flour into a bowl and stir in the sugar. Work in the butter evenly with your fingertips until combined.

2 Beat the egg and orange rind in a bowl, then stir into the mixture to make a firm dough. Add a little water if the mixture is too dry, and knead briefly.

3 Roll out the pastry on a lightly floured surface and use to line a deep, 20 cm / 8 in loose-based flan tin. Chill for 30 minutes.

4 Preheat oven to 180°C / 350°F / Gas 4. Make the filling. Melt the syrup, sugar, chocolate and butter in a small saucepan.

5 Remove the saucepan from the heat and beat in the eggs and vanilla essence. Sprinkle the pecan nuts into the pastry case and carefully pour over the chocolate mixture.

6 Place the tin on a baking sheet and bake the pie for 50–60 minutes or until the filling is set. Leave in the tin for 10 minutes, then remove the sides to serve. Serve plain, or with a little single cream.

CHOCOLATE AMARETTI PEACHES

SERVES 4

115g/4oz amaretti biscuits, crushed
50g/2oz plain chocolate, chopped
grated rind of ½ orange
15ml/1 tbsp clear honey
1.5ml/¼ tsp ground cinnamon
1 egg white, lightly beaten
4 firm ripe peaches
150ml/¼ pint/⅔ cup white wine
15ml/1 tbsp caster sugar
whipped cream, to serve

1 Preheat oven to 190°C/375°F/Gas 5. Mix together the crushed amaretti biscuits, chocolate, orange rind, honey and cinnamon in a bowl. Add the beaten egg white and mix to bind the mixture.

2 Halve and stone the peaches and fill the cavities with the chocolate mixture, mounding it up slightly.

3 Arrange the stuffed peaches in a lightly buttered, shallow ovenproof dish, which will just hold the peaches comfortably. Mix the wine and sugar in a jug.

4 Pour the wine mixture around the peaches. Bake for 30–40 minutes, until the peaches are tender when tested with a slim metal skewer and the filling is golden. Serve at once with a little of the cooking juices spooned over. Offer the whipped cream separately.

PEACHY CHOCOLATE BAKE

SERVES 6

*200g/7oz plain dark chocolate, chopped into
small pieces
115g/4oz/½ cup unsalted butter
4 eggs, separated
115g/4oz/½ cup caster sugar
425g/15oz can peach slices, drained
whipped cream or Greek-style yogurt,
to serve*

1 Preheat oven to 160°C/325°F/Gas 3.
Butter a wide ovenproof dish. Melt the
chocolate with the butter in a heatproof
bowl over barely simmering water.
Remove from the heat.

2 Whisk the egg yolks with the sugar
until thick and pale. In a clean, grease-
free bowl, whisk the whites until stiff.

3 Beat the chocolate into the egg yolk
mixture. Fold in the whites lightly.

4 Fold the peach slices into the mixture,
then tip into the prepared dish. Bake for
35–40 minutes or until risen and just
firm. Serve hot, with cream or Greek-
style yogurt if liked.

CHOCOLATE AND ORANGE SCOTCH PANCAKES

SERVES 4
115g/4oz/1 cup self-raising flour
30ml/2 tbsp cocoa powder
2 eggs
50g/2oz plain chocolate, chopped into
small pieces
200ml/7fl oz/scant 1 cup milk
finely grated rind of 1 orange
30ml/2 tbsp orange juice
butter or oil, for frying
chocolate curls, to decorate

FOR THE SAUCE
2 large oranges
25g/1oz/2 tbsp unsalted butter
45ml/3 tbsp light muscovado sugar
250ml/8fl oz/1 cup crème fraîche
30ml/2 tbsp Grand Marnier or
Cointreau

1 Sift the flour and cocoa into a bowl and make a well in the centre. Add the eggs and beat well, gradually incorporating the surrounding dry ingredients to make a smooth mixture.

2 Mix the chocolate and milk in a saucepan. Heat gently until the chocolate has melted, then beat into the mixture until smooth and bubbly. Stir in the orange rind and juice to make a batter.

3 Heat a large heavy-based frying pan or griddle. Grease with a little butter or oil. Drop large spoonfuls of batter on to the hot surface, leaving room for spreading. Cook over a moderate heat. When the pancakes are lightly browned underneath and bubbly on top, flip over to cook the other side. Slide on to a plate and keep hot, then make more in the same way.

4 Make the sauce. Grate the rind of 1 orange into a bowl and set aside. Peel both oranges, taking care to remove all the pith, then slice the flesh fairly thinly.

5 Heat the butter and sugar in a wide, shallow pan over a low heat, stirring until the sugar dissolves. Stir in the crème fraîche and heat gently.

6 Add the pancakes and orange slices to the sauce, heat gently for 1–2 minutes, then spoon over the liqueur. Sprinkle with the reserved orange rind. Scatter over the chocolate curls and serve the pancakes at once.

RICH CHOCOLATE BRIOCHE BAKE

SERVES 4

40g / 1½oz / 3 tbsp unsalted butter, plus extra
for greasing
200g / 7oz plain chocolate, chopped into
small pieces
60ml / 4 tbsp bitter marmalade
4 individual brioches, cut into halves, or
1 large brioche loaf, cut into
thick slices
3 eggs
300ml / ½ pint / 1¼ cups milk
300ml / ½ pint / 1¼ cups single cream
30ml / 2 tbsp demerara sugar

1 Preheat oven to 180°C / 350°F / Gas 4. Using the extra butter, lightly grease a shallow ovenproof dish.

2 Melt the chocolate with the marmalade and butter in a heatproof bowl over just simmering water, stirring the mixture occasionally, until smooth.

3 Spread the melted chocolate mixture over the brioche slices. Arrange them in the dish so that the slices overlap.

4 Beat the eggs in a large bowl, then add the milk and cream and mix well. Transfer to a jug and pour evenly over the slices. Sprinkle with the demerara sugar and bake for 40–50 minutes, until the custard has set lightly and the brioche slices are golden brown. Serve hot.

CHOCOLATE ORANGE MARQUISE

SERVES 6–8

200g/7oz/scant 1 cup caster sugar
60ml/4 tbsp freshly squeezed orange juice
350g/12oz plain dark chocolate, chopped
into small pieces
225g/8oz/1 cup unsalted butter, cubed
5 eggs
finely grated rind of 1 orange
45ml/3 tbsp plain flour
icing sugar and finely pared strips of orange
rind, to decorate

<u>1</u> Preheat oven to 180°C/350°F/Gas 4.
Grease a 23 cm/9 in round cake tin with
a depth of 6 cm/2½ in. Line the base
with non-stick baking paper.
<u>2</u> Place 115g/4oz/½ cup of the sugar in a
saucepan. Add the orange juice and stir
over a gentle heat until the sugar has
dissolved completely.

<u>3</u> Remove from the heat and stir in the
chocolate until melted, then add the
butter, cube by cube, until thoroughly
melted and evenly mixed.
<u>4</u> Whisk the eggs with the remaining
sugar in a large bowl until pale and very
thick. Add the orange rind. Then, using a
metal spoon, fold the chocolate mixture
lightly and evenly into the egg mixture.
Sift the flour over the top and fold in.

<u>5</u> Scrape the mixture into the prepared
tin. Place in a roasting pan, transfer to
the oven, then carefully pour hot water
into the roasting pan to come about
halfway up the sides of the cake tin.
<u>6</u> Bake for about 1 hour or until the cake
is firm to the touch. Remove the cake tin
from the water bath and place on a wire
rack to cool for 15–20 minutes. To turn
out, invert the cake on a baking sheet,
place a serving plate upside down on top,
then turn plate and baking sheet over
together so that the cake is transferred to
the plate.
<u>7</u> Dust with icing sugar, decorate with
strips of pared orange rind and serve still
warm. This cake is wonderfully rich and
moist and really doesn't need an
accompaniment, but you could offer
single cream, if you wish.

HOT CHOCOLATE ZABAGLIONE

SERVES 6

6 egg yolks
150g / 5oz / ⅔ cup caster sugar
45ml / 3 tbsp cocoa powder
200ml / 7fl oz / scant 1 cup Marsala
cocoa powder or icing sugar, for dusting

2 Add the cocoa and Marsala, then place the bowl over the simmering water. Whisk with a hand-held electric mixer until the mixture is thick and foamy.

3 Pour quickly into tall heatproof glasses, dust lightly with cocoa or icing sugar and serve immediately with chocolate cinnamon tuiles or amaretti biscuits.

1 Half fill a medium saucepan with water and bring to simmering point. Select a heatproof bowl that will fit over the pan, place the egg yolks and sugar in it, and whisk until the mixture is pale and all the sugar has dissolved.

CHOCOLATE FONDUE
SERVES 4-6

225g / 8oz plain chocolate, chopped into small pieces
300ml / ½ pint / 1¼ cups double cream
30ml / 2 tbsp Grand Marnier (optional)
25g / 1oz / 2 tbsp butter, diced
cherries, strawberries, sliced bananas, mandarin segments and cubes of sponge cake, for dipping

1 Combine the chocolate, cream and Grand Marnier (if using) in a fondue pan or small heavy-based saucepan. Heat gently until melted, stirring frequently.
2 Arrange the fruit and cake for dipping on a large platter. Stir the butter into the fondue until melted. Place the fondue pot or pan over a lighted spirit burner.
3 Guests spear the items of their choice on fondue forks and swirl them in the dip until coated. Anyone who loses his or her dipper pays a forfeit.

CHOCOLATE TARTS, PIES AND CHEESECAKES

GREEK CHOCOLATE MOUSSE TARTLETS

SERVES 6

1 quantity Chocolate Shortcrust Pastry
chocolate shapes, to decorate
FOR THE FILLING
200g/7oz white chocolate, chopped into
small pieces
120ml/4fl oz/½ cup milk
10ml/2 tsp powdered gelatine
30ml/2 tbsp caster sugar
5ml/1 tsp vanilla essence
2 eggs, separated
250ml/8fl oz/1 cup Greek-style yogurt

1 Preheat oven to 190°C/375°F/Gas 5. Roll out the pastry and line six deep 10 cm/4 in loose-based flan tins.

2 Prick the pastry with a fork, cover with greaseproof paper weighed down with baking beans and bake blind for 10 minutes. Remove the baking beans and paper, return to the oven and bake a further 15 minutes. Cool in the tins.

3 Make the filling. Melt the chocolate. Pour the milk into a saucepan, sprinkle over the powdered gelatine and heat gently, stirring until the gelatine has dissolved completely. Remove from the heat and stir in the chocolate.

4 Whisk the sugar, vanilla essence and egg yolks in a large bowl, then beat in the chocolate mixture. Beat in the yogurt until evenly mixed.

5 Whisk the egg whites in a clean, grease-free bowl until stiff, then fold into the mixture. Divide among the pastry cases and chill for 2–3 hours, until set. Decorate with chocolate shapes, and dust with icing sugar if wished.

CHOCOLATE TRUFFLE TART

SERVES 12

115g/4oz/1 cup plain flour
30g/1¼oz/⅓ cup cocoa powder
50g/2oz/¼ cup caster sugar
2.5ml/½ tsp salt
115g/4oz/½ cup unsalted butter, cut
into pieces
1 egg yolk
15—30ml/1—2 tbsp iced water
25g/1oz fine quality white or milk chocolate,
melted
whipped cream for serving (optional)
FOR THE TRUFFLE FILLING
350ml/12fl oz/1½ cups double cream
350g/12oz couverture or fine quality
bittersweet chocolate, chopped
50g/2oz/4 tbsp unsalted butter, cut into
small pieces
30ml/2 tbsp brandy or liqueur

1 Prepare the pastry. Sift the flour and cocoa into a bowl. In a food processor fitted with a metal blade, process the flour mixture with the sugar and salt. Add the butter and process for 15–20 seconds, until the mixture resembles coarse breadcrumbs.

2 In a bowl, lightly beat the yolk with the iced water. Add to the flour mixture and pulse until the dough begins to stick together. Turn out the dough on to a sheet of clear film. Use the film to help shape the dough into a flat disc. Wrap tightly. Chill for 1–2 hours, until firm.

3 Lightly grease a 23 cm/9 in tart tin with a removable base. Let the dough soften briefly, then roll it out between sheets of waxed paper or clear film to a 28 cm/11 in round, about 5 mm/¼ in thick. Peel off the top sheet and invert the dough into a tart tin. Remove the bottom sheet. Ease the dough into the tin. Prick with a fork. Chill for 1 hour.

4 Preheat oven to 180°C/350°F/Gas 4. Line the tart with foil or non-stick baking paper; fill with baking beans. Bake blind for 5–7 minutes. Lift out the foil with the beans, return the pastry case to the oven and bake for a further 5–7 minutes, until the pastry is just set. Cool completely in the tin on a rack.

5 Prepare the filling. In a medium pan over a medium heat, bring the cream to the boil. Remove the pan from the heat and stir in the chocolate until melted and smooth. Stir in the butter and brandy or liqueur. Strain into the prepared tart shell, tilting the tin slightly to level the surface. Do not touch the surface of the filling or it will spoil the glossy finish.

6 Spoon the melted chocolate into a paper piping bag and cut off the tip. Drop rounds of chocolate over the surface of the tart and use a skewer or toothpick to draw a point gently through the chocolate to produce a marbled effect. Chill for 2–3 hours, until set. To serve, allow the tart to soften slightly at room temperature.

BAKED CHOCOLATE AND RAISIN CHEESECAKE

SERVES 8–10

75g/3oz/¾ cup plain flour
45ml/3 tbsp cocoa powder
75g/3oz/½ cup semolina
50g/2oz/¼ cup caster sugar
115g/4oz/½ cup unsalted butter, softened

FOR THE FILLING

225g/8oz/1 cup cream cheese
120ml/4fl oz/½ cup natural yogurt
2 eggs, beaten
75g/3oz/6 tbsp caster sugar
finely grated rind of 1 lemon
75g/3oz/½ cup raisins
45ml/3 tbsp plain chocolate chips

FOR THE TOPPING

75g/3oz plain chocolate, chopped into
small pieces
30ml/2 tbsp golden syrup
40g/1½oz/3 tbsp butter

<u>1</u> Preheat oven to 150°C/300°F/Gas 2. Sift the flour and cocoa into a mixing bowl and stir in the semolina and sugar. Using your fingertips, work the butter into the flour mixture until it makes a firm dough.

<u>2</u> Press the dough into the base of a 22 cm/8½ in springform tin. Prick all over with a fork and bake in the oven for 15 minutes. Remove the tin but leave the oven on.

RUM AND RICOTTA CHEESECAKE

Use ricotta instead of cream cheese in the filling. Omit the lemon rind. Soak the raisins in 30ml/2 tbsp rum before stirring them in with the chocolate chips. Add 5ml/1 tsp rum to the topping.

<u>3</u> Make the filling. In a large bowl, beat the cream cheese with the yogurt, eggs and sugar until evenly mixed. Stir in the lemon rind, raisins and chocolate chips.

<u>4</u> Smooth the cream cheese mixture over the chocolate shortbread base and bake for a further 35–45 minutes or until the filling is pale gold and just set. Cool in the tin on a wire rack.

<u>5</u> To make the topping, combine the chocolate, syrup and butter in a heatproof bowl. Set over a saucepan of simmering water and heat gently, stirring occasionally, until melted. Pour the topping over the cheesecake and leave until set. Remove the sides of the tin and carefully slide the chocolate and raisin cheesecake on to a serving plate. Serve sliced, with single cream, if you like.

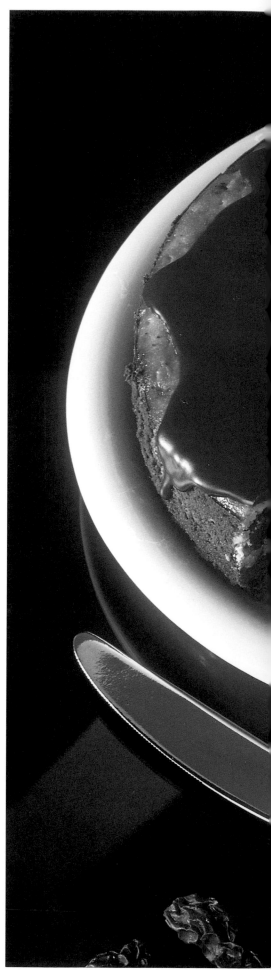

WHITE CHOCOLATE AND MANGO CREAM TART

SERVES 8

175g/6oz/1½ cups plain flour
75g/3oz/1 cup sweetened, desiccated coconut
115g/4oz/½ cup butter, softened
30ml/2 tbsp caster sugar
2 egg yolks
2.5ml/½ tsp almond essence
600ml/1 pint/2½ cups whipping cream
1 large ripe mango
50g/2oz/½ cup toasted flaked almonds,
to decorate

FOR THE WHITE CHOCOLATE
CUSTARD FILLING

150g/5oz fine quality white chocolate,
chopped into small pieces
120ml/4fl oz/½ cup whipping cream or
double cream
75ml/5 tbsp cornflour
15ml/1 tbsp plain flour
50g/2oz/¼ cup granulated sugar
350ml/12fl oz/1½ cups milk
5 egg yolks

1 Using a hand-held electric mixer at low speed, beat the flour, coconut, butter, sugar, egg yolks and almond essence in a deep bowl until the mixture forms a soft dough. Lightly grease a 23 cm/9 in tart tin with a removable base. Press the pastry on to the bottom and sides. Prick the pastry case with a fork. Chill the case for 30 minutes.

COOK'S TIP

Choose a mango that is a rich yellow in colour, with a pink or red blush. It should just yield to the touch, but should not be too soft. Peel it carefully, then cut it in half around the stone. Cut each piece in half again, then in neat slices.

2 Preheat oven to 180°C/350°F/Gas 4. Line the pastry case with non-stick baking paper; fill with baking beans and bake blind for 10 minutes. Remove the paper and beans and bake for a further 5–7 minutes, until golden. Cool the cooked pastry in the tin on a wire rack.

3 Prepare the custard filling. In a small saucepan over a low heat, melt the white chocolate with the cream, stirring until smooth. Set aside. Combine the cornflour, plain flour and sugar in a medium saucepan. Stir in the milk gradually. Place over a medium heat and cook, stirring constantly, until the mixture has thickened.

4 Beat the egg yolks in a small bowl. Slowly add about 250ml/8fl oz/1 cup of the hot milk mixture, stirring constantly. Return the yolk mixture to the rest of the sauce in the pan, stirring constantly.

5 Bring the custard filling to a gentle boil, stirring constantly until thickened. Stir in the melted white chocolate until well blended. Cool to room temperature, stirring frequently to prevent a skin from forming on the surface. Beat the whipping cream in a medium-sized bowl until soft peaks form. Fold approximately 120ml/4fl oz/½ cup of the whipped cream into the white chocolate custard and spoon half the custard into the base. Peel and slice the mango thinly.

6 With the aid of a slim metal spatula or palette knife, arrange the mango slices over the custard in concentric circles, starting at the rim and then filling in the centre. Try to avoid moving the mango slices once in position. Carefully pour the remaining custard over the mango slices, smoothing the surface evenly. Remove the side of the tin and slide the tart carefully on to a serving plate.

7 Spoon the remaining flavoured cream into a large piping bag fitted with a medium star tip. Pipe the cream in a scroll pattern in parallel rows on top of the tart, keeping the rows about 1 cm/½ in apart. Carefully sprinkle the toasted flaked almonds between the rows. Serve the tart chilled.

CHOCOLATE PECAN TORTE

SERVES 16

200g/7oz bittersweet or plain chocolate,
chopped into small pieces
150g/5oz/10 tbsp unsalted butter,
cut into pieces
4 eggs
90g/3½oz/scant ½ cup caster sugar
10ml/2 tsp vanilla essence
115g/4oz/1 cup ground pecan nuts
10ml/2 tsp ground cinnamon
24 toasted pecan halves, to decorate

FOR THE CHOCOLATE HONEY GLAZE

115g/4oz bittersweet or plain chocolate,
chopped into small pieces
50g/2oz/¼ cup unsalted butter,
cut into pieces
30ml/2 tbsp clear honey
pinch of ground cinnamon

1 Preheat oven to 180°C/350°F/Gas 4. Grease a 20 x 5 cm/8 x 2 in springform tin; line with non-stick baking paper. Wrap the tin in foil to prevent water from seeping in. Melt the chocolate and butter, stirring until smooth. Beat the eggs, sugar and vanilla essence in a mixing bowl until the mixture is frothy. Stir in the melted chocolate, ground nuts and cinnamon. Pour into the tin.

2 Place the tin in a roasting pan. Pour in boiling water to come 2 cm/¾ in up the side of the springform tin. Bake for 25–30 minutes, until the edge of the cake is set but the centre is still soft. Remove the tin from the water bath and lift off the foil. Cool the cake in the tin on a wire rack.

3 Prepare the glaze. Heat all the ingredients in a small pan until melted, stirring until smooth. Off the heat, half-dip the toasted pecan halves in the glaze and place on a baking sheet lined with non-stick baking paper until set.

4 Remove the cake from the tin, place it on the rack and pour the remaining glaze over. Decorate the outside of the torte with the chocolate-dipped pecans and leave to set. Transfer to a plate when ready to serve, and slice in thin wedges.

CHOCOLATE LEMON TART

SERVES 8–10

175g/6oz/1½ cups plain flour
10ml/2 tsp cocoa powder
25g/1oz/¼ cup icing sugar
2.5ml/½ tsp salt
115g/4oz/½ cup unsalted butter or
margarine
15ml/1 tbsp water
FOR THE FILLING
225g/8oz/1 cup caster sugar
6 eggs
grated rind of 2 lemons
175ml/6fl oz/¾ cup fresh lemon juice
175ml/6fl oz/¾ cup double or
whipping cream
chocolate curls, for decorating

1 Grease a 25 cm/10 in flan tin. Sift the flour, cocoa, icing sugar and salt into a bowl. Set aside. Melt the butter or margarine and water in a saucepan over a low heat. Pour over the flour mixture and stir until the flour has absorbed all the liquid and the dough is smooth.

2 Press the dough evenly over the base and side of the prepared tin. Chill the pastry case.

3 Preheat oven to 190°C/375°F/Gas 5, and place a baking sheet inside to heat up. Prepare the filling. Whisk the sugar and eggs in a bowl until the sugar has dissolved. Add the lemon rind and juice and mix well. Stir in the cream. Taste and add more lemon juice or sugar if needed, for a sweet taste with a touch of tartness.

4 Pour the filling into the tart shell and place the tin on the hot baking sheet. Bake for 20–25 minutes or until the filling is set. Cool on a rack, then decorate with the chocolate curls.

CHOCOLATE APRICOT LINZER TART

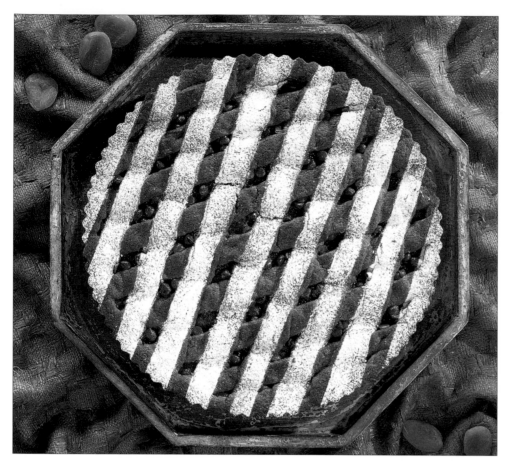

3 Turn the dough on to a flour-dusted work surface and knead lightly until just blended. Divide the dough in half. With floured fingers, press half the dough on to the bottom and sides of the tin. Prick the base of the dough with a fork. Chill for 20 minutes. Roll out the rest of the dough between two sheets of non-stick baking paper or clear film to a 28 cm/11 in round; slide on to a baking sheet and chill for 30 minutes.

SERVES 10–12

50g/2oz/½ cup whole blanched almonds
115g/4oz/½ cup caster sugar
175g/6oz/1½ cups plain flour
30ml/2 tbsp cocoa powder
5ml/1 tsp ground cinnamon
2.5ml/½ tsp salt
5ml/1 tsp grated orange rind
225g/8oz/1 cup unsalted butter, cut into small pieces
45–60ml/3–4 tbsp iced water
75g/3oz/½ cup plain mini chocolate chips
icing sugar, for dusting

FOR THE APRICOT FILLING

350g/12oz/1½ cups dried apricots
120ml/4fl oz/½ cup orange juice
175ml/6fl oz/¾ cup water
45ml/3 tbsp granulated sugar
50g/2oz/2 tbsp apricot jam
2.5ml/½ tsp almond essence

2 Prepare the pastry. Lightly grease a 28 cm/11 in tart tin with removable base. In a food processor with a metal blade, process the almonds with half the sugar until finely ground. Into a bowl, sift the flour, cocoa, cinnamon and salt. Stir in the remaining caster sugar. Add to the food processor and process to blend. Add the rind and butter and process for 15–20 seconds until the mixture resembles coarse crumbs. Add about 30ml/2 tbsp iced water and pulse until the dough just begins to stick together. If the dough appears too dry, add 15–30ml/1–2 tbsp more iced water, little by little, until the dough just holds together.

4 Preheat oven to 180°C/350°F/Gas 4. Spread the filling on to the base of the pastry-lined tin. Sprinkle with chocolate chips. Set aside. Slide the dough round on to a lightly floured surface and cut into 1 cm/½ in strips; allow the strips to soften for 3–5 minutes so that they will be easier to work with.

5 Place half the dough strips over the filling, spacing them about 1 cm/½ in apart. Place the rest of the strips at an angle on top, as shown. With your fingertips, press down on both sides of each crossing to stress the lattice effect. Press the ends on to the side of the tart, cutting off any excess. Bake for 35–40 minutes, until the strips are golden and the filling bubbles. Cool on a rack. To serve, remove the side of the tin, then dust icing sugar over the top pastry strips.

1 Prepare the filling. In a pan, simmer the apricots, orange juice and water until the liquid is absorbed, stirring often. Stir in the remaining ingredients. Strain into a bowl, cool, cover and chill.

RICH CHOCOLATE BERRY TART WITH BLACKBERRY SAUCE

SERVES 10

115g/4oz/½ cup unsalted butter, softened
115g/4oz/½ cup caster sugar
2.5ml/½ tsp salt
15ml/1 tbsp vanilla essence
50g/2oz/½ cup cocoa powder
175g/6oz/1½ cups plain flour
450g/1 lb fresh berries, for topping

FOR THE CHOCOLATE GANACHE FILLING

475ml/16fl oz/2 cups double cream
150g/5oz/½ cup blackberry or raspberry jelly
225g/8oz bittersweet chocolate, chopped into small pieces
25g/1oz/2 tbsp unsalted butter, cut into small pieces

FOR THE BLACKBERRY SAUCE

225g/8oz fresh or frozen blackberries or raspberries
15ml/1 tbsp lemon juice
30ml/2 tbsp caster sugar
30ml/2 tbsp blackberry- or raspberry-flavoured liqueur

1 In a food processor fitted with a metal blade, process the butter, sugar, salt and vanilla essence until creamy. Add the cocoa and process for 1 minute. Add the flour all at once, then pulse for 10–15 seconds. Place a piece of clear film on the work surface. Turn the dough out on to this, shape into a flat disc and wrap tightly. Chill for 1 hour.

2 Lightly grease a 23 cm/9 in flan tin with a removable base. Let the dough soften for 5–10 minutes, then roll out between two sheets of clear film to a 28 cm/11 in round, about 5 mm/¼ in thick. Peel off the top sheet of clear film and invert the dough into the prepared tin. Ease the dough into the tin, and when in position lift off the clear film.

3 With floured fingers, press the dough on to the base and sides of the tin, then roll the rolling pin over the edge to cut off any excess dough. Prick the base of the dough with a fork. Chill for 1 hour. Preheat oven to 180°C/350°F/Gas 4. Line the pastry case with non-stick baking paper; fill with baking beans and bake blind for 10 minutes. Remove the paper and beans and bake for 5 minutes more, until the pastry is just set. Cool in the tin on a wire rack.

4 Prepare the ganache filling. In a medium saucepan over a medium heat, bring the cream and berry jelly to the boil. Remove from the heat and add the chocolate all at once, stirring until melted and smooth. Stir in the butter until melted, then strain into the cooled tart shell, smoothing the top. Cool the tart completely.

5 Prepare the sauce. Process the berries, lemon juice and sugar in a food processor until smooth. Strain into a small bowl and add the liqueur.

6 To serve, remove the tart from the tin. Place on a serving plate and arrange the berries on top of the tart. With a pastry brush, brush the berries with a little of the blackberry sauce to glaze lightly. Serve the remaining sauce separately.

BAKED CHOCOLATE CHEESECAKE

SERVES 10–12

*275g/10oz plain chocolate, chopped into
small pieces
1.2kg/2½lb/5 cups cream cheese, at room
temperature
200g/7oz/scant 1 cup granulated sugar
10ml/2 tsp vanilla essence
4 eggs, at room temperature
175ml/6fl oz/¾ cup soured cream
15ml/1 tbsp cocoa powder*

FOR THE BASE

*200g/7oz chocolate biscuits, crushed
75g/3oz/6 tbsp butter, melted
2.5ml/½ tsp ground cinnamon*

1 Preheat oven to 180°C/350°F/Gas 4.
Lightly grease the base and sides of a
23 x 7.5 cm/9 x 3 in springform tin.

2 To make the base, mix the crushed
biscuits with the butter and cinnamon.
Press the mixture evenly on to the base of
the tin to make a crust. Melt the
chocolate and set it aside.

3 Beat the cream cheese until smooth,
then beat in the sugar and vanilla essence.
Add the eggs, one at a time.

4 Stir the soured cream into the cocoa
powder to form a paste. Add to the
cream cheese mixture. Stir in the melted
chocolate and mix until smooth.

5 Pour the filling on to the base. Bake for
1 hour. Cool in the tin, then remove the
sides of the tin and slide the cheesecake
on to a plate. Serve chilled.

MARBLED CHOCOLATE CHEESECAKE

SERVES 6

50g/2oz/½ cup cocoa powder
75ml/5 tbsp hot water
900g/2lb cream cheese, at room temperature
200g/7oz/scant 1 cup caster sugar
4 eggs
5ml/1 tsp vanilla essence
75g/3oz digestive biscuits, crushed

<u>1</u> Preheat oven to 180°C/350°F/Gas 4. Line a 20 x 8 cm/8 x 3 in cake tin with greaseproof paper. Grease the paper.
<u>2</u> Sift the cocoa powder into a bowl. Pour over the hot water and stir to dissolve.
<u>3</u> Beat the cheese until smooth, then beat in the sugar, followed by the eggs, one at a time. Do not overmix.
<u>4</u> Divide the mixture evenly between two bowls. Stir the chocolate mixture into one bowl, then add the vanilla essence to the remaining mixture.

<u>5</u> Pour a cup or ladleful of the plain mixture into the centre of the tin; it will spread out into an even layer. Slowly pour over a cupful of chocolate mixture in the centre. Continue to alternate the cake mixtures in this way until both are used up. Draw a thin metal skewer through the cake mixture for a marbled effect.
<u>6</u> Set the tin in a roasting pan and pour in hot water to come 4 cm/1½ in up the sides of the cake tin.

<u>7</u> Bake the cheesecake for about 1½ hours, until the top is golden. (The cake will rise during baking but will sink later.) Cool in the tin on a wire rack.
<u>8</u> Run a knife around the inside edge of the cake. Invert a flat plate over the tin and turn out the cake.

<u>9</u> Sprinkle the crushed biscuits evenly over the cake, gently invert another plate on top, and turn over again. Cover and chill for 3 hours, preferably overnight.

RASPBERRY, MASCARPONE AND WHITE CHOCOLATE CHEESECAKE

SERVES 8

50g / 2oz / ¼ cup unsalted butter
225g / 8oz ginger biscuits, crushed
50g / 2oz / ½ cup chopped pecan nuts
or walnuts

FOR THE FILLING

275g / 10oz / 1¼ cups mascarpone cheese
175g / 6oz / ¾ cup fromage frais
2 eggs, beaten
45ml / 3 tbsp caster sugar
250g / 9oz white chocolate, chopped into
small pieces
225g / 8oz / 1½ cups fresh or frozen raspberries

FOR THE TOPPING

115g / 4oz / ½ cup mascarpone cheese
75g / 3oz / ⅓ cup fromage frais
white chocolate curls and fresh raspberries,
to decorate

1 Preheat oven to 150°C/300°F/Gas 2. Melt the butter in a saucepan, then stir in the crushed biscuits and nuts. Press into the base of a 23 cm/9 in springform cake tin. Level the surface.

2 Make the filling. Using a wooden spoon, beat the mascarpone and fromage frais in a large mixing bowl, then beat in the eggs, a little at a time. Add the caster sugar. Beat until the sugar has dissolved, and the mixture is smooth and creamy.

3 Melt the white chocolate gently in a heatproof bowl over a saucepan of simmering water, then stir into the cheese mixture. Add the fresh or frozen raspberries and mix lightly.

4 Tip into the prepared tin and spread evenly, then bake for about 1 hour or until just set. Switch off the oven, but do not remove the cheesecake. Leave it until cold and completely set.

5 Remove the sides of the tin and carefully lift the cheesecake on to a serving plate. Make the topping by mixing the mascarpone and fromage frais in a bowl and spreading the mixture over the cheesecake. Decorate with chocolate curls and raspberries.

APRICOT AND WHITE CHOCOLATE CHEESECAKE

Use 225g/8oz/1 cup ready-to-eat dried apricots instead of the fresh or frozen raspberries in the cheesecake mixture. Slice the apricots thinly or dice them. Omit the mascarpone and fromage frais topping and serve the cheesecake with an apricot sauce, made by poaching 225g/8oz stoned fresh apricots in 120ml/4fl oz/½ cup water until tender, then rubbing the fruit and liquid through a sieve placed over a bowl. Sweeten the apricot purée with caster sugar to taste, and add enough lemon juice to sharpen the flavour. Alternatively, purée drained canned apricots with a little of their syrup, then stir in lemon juice to taste.

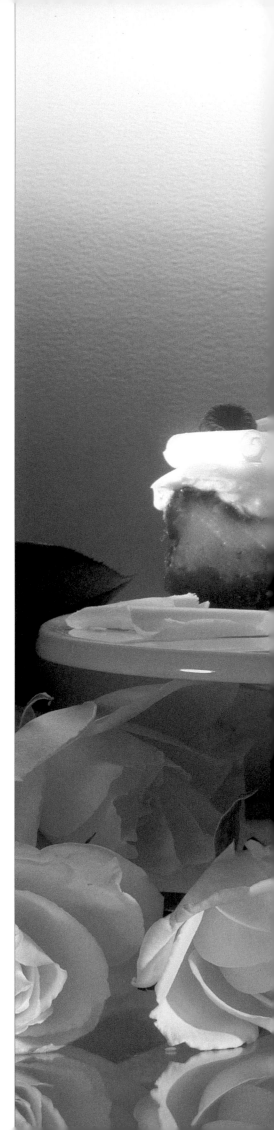

LUXURY WHITE CHOCOLATE CHEESECAKE

SERVES 16–20

150g/5oz (about 16–18) digestive biscuits
50g/2oz/½ cup blanched hazelnuts, toasted
50g/2oz/¼ cup unsalted butter, melted
2.5ml/½ tsp ground cinnamon
white chocolate curls, to decorate
cocoa powder, for dusting (optional)

FOR THE FILLING

350g/12oz fine quality white chocolate,
chopped into small pieces
120ml/4fl oz/½ cup whipping cream or
double cream
675g/1½lb/3 x 8oz packets cream
cheese, softened
50g/2oz/¼ cup granulated sugar
4 eggs
30ml/2 tbsp hazelnut-flavoured liqueur or
15ml/1 tbsp vanilla essence

FOR THE TOPPING

450ml/¾ pint/1¾ cups soured cream
50g/2oz/¼ cup granulated sugar
15ml/1 tbsp hazelnut-flavoured liqueur or
5ml/1 tsp vanilla essence

3 Using a hand-held electric mixer, beat the cream cheese and sugar in a large bowl until smooth. Add the eggs one at a time, beating well. Slowly beat in the white chocolate mixture and liqueur or vanilla essence. Pour the filling into the baked crust. Place the tin on the hot baking sheet. Bake for 45–55 minutes, and do not allow the top to brown. Transfer the cheesecake to a wire rack while preparing the topping. Increase the oven temperature to 200°C/400°F/Gas 6.

4 Prepare the topping. In a small bowl whisk the soured cream, sugar and liqueur or vanilla essence until thoroughly mixed. Pour the mixture over the cheesecake, spreading it evenly, and return to the oven. Bake for a further 5–7 minutes. Turn off the oven, but do not open the door for 1 hour. Serve the cheesecake at room temperature, decorated with the white chocolate curls. Dust the surface lightly with cocoa powder, if desired.

1 Preheat oven to 180°C/350°F/Gas 4. Grease a 23 x 7.5 cm/9 x 3 in springform tin. In a food processor, process the biscuits and hazelnuts until fine crumbs form. Pour in the butter and cinnamon. Process just until blended. Using the back of a spoon, press on to the base and to within 1 cm/½ in of the top of the sides of the cake tin. Bake the crumb crust for 5–7 minutes, until just set. Cool in the tin on a wire rack. Lower the oven temperature to 150°C/300°F/Gas 2 and place a baking sheet inside to heat up.

2 Prepare the filling. In a small saucepan over a low heat, melt the white chocolate and cream until smooth, stirring frequently. Set aside to cool slightly.

CHOCOLATE, BANANA AND TOFFEE PIE

SERVES 6

*65g / 2½oz / 5 tbsp unsalted butter,
melted*

*250g / 9oz milk chocolate digestive biscuits,
crushed*

chocolate curls, to decorate

FOR THE FILLING

397g / 13oz can condensed milk

150g / 5oz plain chocolate, chopped

120ml / 4fl oz / ½ cup crème fraîche

15ml / 1 tbsp golden syrup

FOR THE TOPPING

2 bananas

250ml / 8fl oz / 1 cup crème fraîche

10ml / 2 tsp strong black coffee

<u>1</u> Mix the butter with the biscuit crumbs. Press on to the base and sides of a 23cm / 9in loose-based flan tin. Chill.

<u>2</u> Make the filling. Place the unopened can of condensed milk in a deep saucepan of boiling water, making sure that it is completely covered. Lower the heat and simmer, covered for 2 hours, topping up the water as necessary. The can must remain covered at all times.

<u>3</u> Remove the pan from the heat and set aside, covered, until the can has cooled down completely in the water. Do not attempt to open the can until it is completely cold.

<u>4</u> Gently melt the chocolate with the crème fraîche and golden syrup in a heatproof bowl over a saucepan of simmering water. Stir in the caramelized condensed milk and beat until evenly mixed. Pour the filling into the biscuit crust and spread it evenly.

<u>5</u> Slice the bananas evenly and arrange them over the chocolate filling.

<u>6</u> Stir the crème fraîche and coffee together in a bowl, then spoon the mixture over the bananas. Sprinkle the chocolate curls on top. Alternatively, omit the crème fraîche topping and decorate with whipped cream and extra banana slices.

BLACK BOTTOM PIE

SERVES 6–8

250g/9oz/2¼ cups plain flour
150g/5oz/⅔ cup unsalted butter
2 egg yolks
15–30ml/1–2 tbsp iced water
FOR THE FILLING
3 eggs, separated
20ml/4 tsp cornflour
75g/3oz/6 tbsp golden caster sugar
400ml/14fl oz/1⅔ cups milk
150g/5oz plain chocolate, chopped into
small pieces
5ml/1 tsp vanilla essence
1 sachet powdered gelatine
45ml/3 tbsp water
30ml/2 tbsp dark rum
FOR THE TOPPING
175ml/6 fl oz/¾ cup double cream or
whipping cream
chocolate curls

1 Sift the flour into a bowl and rub in the butter until the mixture resembles coarse breadcrumbs. Stir in the egg yolks with just enough iced water to bind the mixture to a soft dough. Roll out on a lightly floured surface and line a deep 23 cm/9 in flan tin. Chill the pastry case for about 30 minutes.
2 Preheat oven to 190°C/375°F/Gas 5. Prick the pastry case all over with a fork, cover with greaseproof paper weighed down with baking beans and bake blind for 10 minutes. Remove the baking beans and paper, return the pastry case to the oven and bake for a further 10 minutes, until the pastry is crisp and golden. Cool in the tin.

POTS AU CHOCOLAT
The chocolate and chestnut mixture (minus the pastry) also makes delicious individual *pots au chocolat*. Make the fillings as described above, then simply pour the mixture into small ramekins that have been lightly greased with butter. Decorate with a blob of whipped cream and grated chocolate and serve with *langues de chat*.

CHOCOLATE AND CHESTNUT PIE
23 cm/9 in pastry case (see recipe above), cooked
FOR THE FILLING
115g/4oz/½ cup butter, softened
115g/4oz/¼ cup caster sugar
425g/15oz can unsweetened chestnut purée
225g/8oz plain chocolate, broken into small pieces
30ml/2 tbsp brandy

1 Make the filling. Cream the butter with the caster sugar in a mixing bowl until pale and fluffy. Add the unsweetened chestnut purée, about 30ml/2 tbsp at a time, beating well after each addition.
2 Put the chocolate in a heatproof bowl. Place over a saucepan of barely simmering water until the chocolate has melted, stirring occasionally until smooth. Stir the chocolate into the chestnut mixture until combined, then add the brandy.
3 Pour the filling into the cold pastry case. Using a spatula, level the surface. Chill until set. Decorate with whipped cream and chocolate leaves, if desired, or simply add a dusting of sifted cocoa.

3 Make the filling. Mix the egg yolks, cornflour and 30ml/2 tbsp of the sugar in a bowl. Heat the milk in a saucepan until almost boiling, then beat into the egg mixture. Return to the clean pan and stir over a low heat until the custard has thickened and is smooth. Pour half the custard into a bowl.

4 Put the chocolate in a heatproof bowl. Place over a saucepan of barely simmering water until the chocolate has melted, stirring occasionally until smooth. Stir the melted chocolate into the custard in the bowl, with the vanilla essence. Spread the filling in the pastry case and cover closely with dampened greaseproof paper or clear film to prevent the formation of a skin. Allow to cool, then chill until set.

5 Sprinkle the gelatine over the water in a bowl, leave until spongy, then place the bowl over a pan of simmering water until all the gelatine has dissolved. Stir into the remaining custard, then add the rum. Whisk the egg whites in a clean, grease-free bowl until peaks form. Whisk in the remaining sugar, a little at a time, until stiff, then fold the egg whites quickly but evenly into the rum-flavoured custard.
6 Spoon the rum-flavoured custard over the chocolate layer in the pastry case. Using a spatula, level the mixture, making sure that none of the chocolate custard is visible. Return the pie to the fridge until the top layer has set, then remove the pie from the tin and place it on a serving plate. Whip the cream, spread it over the pie and sprinkle with chocolate curls, to decorate.

CHILLED DESSERTS, ICES AND SORBETS

DOUBLE CHOCOLATE SNOWBALL

3 Bake for 1¼–1½ hours until the surface is firm and slightly risen, but cracked. The centre will still be wobbly, but will set on cooling. Remove the bowl to a rack to cool to room temperature; the top will sink. Cover the surface of the cake with a dinner plate (to make an even surface for unmoulding); then wrap completely with clear film or foil and chill overnight.

4 To unmould, remove the film or foil, lift off the plate, and place an upturned serving plate over the top of the mould. Invert the mould on to the plate and shake firmly to release the cake. Carefully peel off the foil used for lining the bowl. Cover until ready to decorate.

5 In a food processor fitted with a metal blade, process the white chocolate until fine. Heat 120ml/4fl oz/½ cup of the cream in a small saucepan until just beginning to simmer. With the food processor running, pour the hot cream through the feeder tube and process until the chocolate has melted completely. Strain into a medium bowl and cool to room temperature, stirring occasionally.

6 In another bowl, beat the remaining cream with the electric mixer until soft peaks form. Add the liqueur and beat for 30 seconds or until the cream holds its shape, but is not yet stiff. Fold a spoonful of cream into the chocolate mixture to lighten it, then fold in the rest. Spoon into a piping bag fitted with a star tip and pipe rosettes over the surface of the cake. Dust lightly with cocoa powder to finish the decoration.

SERVES 12–14

350g/12oz bittersweet or plain chocolate, chopped into small pieces
350g/12oz/1¾ cups caster sugar
275g/10oz/1¼ cups unsalted butter, cut into small pieces
8 eggs
60ml/4 tbsp orange-flavoured liqueur or brandy
cocoa powder, for dusting

FOR THE WHITE CHOCOLATE CREAM

200g/7oz fine quality white chocolate, chopped into small pieces
475ml/16fl oz/2 cups double or whipping cream
15ml/1 tbsp orange-flavoured liqueur (optional)

1 Preheat oven to 180°C/350°F/Gas 4. Carefully line a 1.75 litre/3 pint/7½ cup round ovenproof bowl with aluminium foil, smoothing the sides. Melt the bittersweet chocolate in a heatproof bowl over a pan of barely simmering water. Add the caster sugar and stir until the chocolate has melted and the sugar has dissolved. Strain the mixture into a medium bowl.

2 With a hand-held electric mixer at low speed, beat in the butter, then the eggs, one at a time, beating well after each addition. Stir in the liqueur or brandy and pour into the prepared bowl. Tap the sides of the bowl gently to release any large air bubbles.

CHOCOLATE AMARETTO MARQUISE

SERVES 10–12

15ml/1 tbsp flavourless vegetable oil, such as groundnut or sunflower
75g/3oz/7–8 amaretti biscuits, finely crushed
25g/1oz/¼ cup unblanched almonds, toasted and finely chopped
450g/1lb fine quality bittersweet or plain chocolate, chopped into small pieces
75ml/5 tbsp Amaretto liqueur
75ml/5 tbsp golden syrup
475ml/16fl oz/2 cups double cream
cocoa powder, for dusting
FOR THE AMARETTO CREAM
350ml/12fl oz/1½ cups whipping cream or double cream for serving
30–45ml/2–3 tbsp Amaretto di Soronno liqueur

1 Lightly oil a 23 cm/9 in heart-shaped or springform cake tin. Line the bottom with non-stick baking paper and oil the paper. In a small bowl, combine the crushed amaretti biscuits and the chopped almonds. Sprinkle evenly on to the base of the tin.

2 Place the chocolate, Amaretto liqueur and golden syrup in a medium saucepan over a very low heat. Stir frequently until the chocolate is melted and the mixture is smooth. Remove from the heat and allow it to cool for about 6–8 minutes, until the mixture feels just warm to the touch.

3 Pour the cream into a bowl. Whip with a hand-held electric mixer, until it just begins to hold its shape. Stir a large spoonful into the chocolate mixture, to lighten it, then quickly add the remaining cream and gently fold into the chocolate mixture. Pour into the prepared tin, on top of the amaretti and almond mixture. Level the surface. Cover the tin with clear film and chill overnight.

4 To unmould, run a thin-bladed sharp knife under hot water and dry carefully. Run the knife around the edge of the tin to loosen the dessert. Place a serving plate over the tin, then invert to unmould. Carefully peel off the paper, replacing any crust that sticks to it, and dust with cocoa powder. In a bowl, whip the cream and Amaretto liqueur to soft peaks. Serve separately.

CHOCOLATE HAZELNUT GALETTES

SERVES 4

*175g/6oz plain chocolate, chopped into small
pieces
45ml/3 tbsp single cream
30ml/2 tbsp flaked hazelnuts
115g/4oz white chocolate, chopped into small
pieces
175g/6oz/¾ cup fromage frais (8% fat)
15ml/1 tbsp dry sherry
60ml/4 tbsp finely chopped hazelnuts, toasted
physalis (Cape gooseberries), dipped in white
chocolate, to decorate*

1 Melt the plain chocolate in a heatproof
bowl over a saucepan of barely simmering
water, then remove the pan from the heat
and lift off the bowl. Stir the cream into
the melted chocolate. Draw twelve
7.5 cm/3 in circles on sheets of non-stick
baking paper.

2 Turn the baking paper over and spread
the plain chocolate over each marked
circle, covering in a thin, even layer.
Scatter flaked hazelnuts over four of the
circles, then leave until set.

3 Melt the white chocolate in a heatproof
bowl over hot water, then stir in the
fromage frais and dry sherry. Fold in the
chopped, toasted hazelnuts. Leave to cool
until the mixture holds its shape.

4 Remove the plain chocolate rounds
carefully from the paper and sandwich
them together in stacks of three,
spooning the white chocolate hazelnut
cream between the layers and using the
hazelnut-covered rounds on top. Chill
before serving.

5 To serve, place the galettes on
individual plates and decorate with
chocolate-dipped physalis.

CHOCOLATE AND CHESTNUT POTS

SERVES 6

250g/9oz plain chocolate
60ml/4 tbsp Madeira
25g/1oz/2 tbsp butter, diced
2 eggs, separated
225g/8oz/1 cup unsweetened chestnut purée
crème fraîche and chocolate curls, to decorate

1 Make a few chocolate curls for decoration, then break the rest of the chocolate into squares and melt it with the Madeira in a heatproof bowl over a saucepan of barely simmering water. Remove from the heat and add the butter, a few pieces at a time, stirring until melted and smooth.

2 Beat the egg yolks quickly into the mixture, then beat in the chestnut purée, a little at a time, making sure that each addition is absorbed before you add the next, mixing until smooth.

3 Whisk the egg whites in a clean, grease-free bowl until stiff. Stir about 15ml/1 tbsp of the whites into the chestnut mixture to lighten it, then fold in the rest evenly.

4 Spoon the mixture into six small ramekin dishes or custard cups and chill until set. Serve the pots topped with a generous spoonful of crème fraîche or whipped double cream. Decorate with the chocolate curls.

MOCHA VELVET CREAM POTS

SERVES 8

15ml/1 tbsp instant coffee powder
475ml/16fl oz/2 cups milk
75g/3oz/6 tbsp caster sugar
225g/8oz plain chocolate, chopped into small pieces
10ml/2 tsp vanilla essence
30ml/2 tbsp coffee liqueur (optional)
7 egg yolks
whipped cream and crystallized mimosa balls, to decorate

1 Preheat oven to 160°C/325°F/Gas 3. Place eight 120ml/ 4fl oz/½ cup custard cups or ramekins in a roasting tin. Set the tin aside.

2 Put the instant coffee into a saucepan. Stir in the milk, then add the sugar and set the pan over a medium heat. Bring to the boil, stirring constantly, until both the coffee and the sugar have dissolved completely.

3 Remove the pan from the heat and add the chocolate. Stir until it has melted and the sauce is smooth. Stir in the vanilla essence and coffee liqueur, if using.

4 In a bowl, whisk the egg yolks to blend them lightly. Slowly whisk in the chocolate mixture until well mixed, then strain the mixture into a large jug and divide equally among the cups or ramekins. Pour enough boiling water into the roasting tin to come halfway up the sides of the cups or ramekins. Carefully place the roasting tin in the oven.

5 Bake for 30–35 minutes, until the custard is just set and a knife inserted into the custard comes out clean. Remove the cups or ramekins from the roasting tin and allow to cool. Place on a baking sheet, cover and chill completely. Decorate with whipped cream and crystallized mimosa balls, if desired.

TIRAMISU IN CHOCOLATE CUPS

SERVES 6

1 egg yolk
30ml / 2 tbsp caster sugar
2.5ml / ½ tsp vanilla essence
250g / 9oz / generous 1 cup mascarpone cheese
120ml / 4fl oz / ½ cup strong black coffee
15ml / 1 tbsp cocoa powder
30ml / 2 tbsp coffee liqueur
16 amaretti biscuits
cocoa powder, for dusting

FOR THE CHOCOLATE CUPS
175g / 6oz plain chocolate, chopped
25g / 1oz / 2 tbsp unsalted butter

1 Make the chocolate cups. Cut out six 15 cm / 6 in rounds of non-stick baking paper. Melt the chocolate with the butter in a heatproof bowl over a saucepan of simmering water. Stir until smooth, then spread a spoonful of the chocolate mixture over each circle, to within 2 cm / ¾ in of the edge.

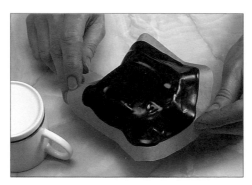

2 Carefully lift each paper round and drape it over an upturned teacup or ramekin so that the edges curve into frills. Leave until completely set, then carefully lift off and peel away the paper to reveal the chocolate cups.

3 Make the filling. Using a hand-held electric mixer, beat the egg yolk and sugar in a bowl until smooth, then stir in the vanilla essence. Soften the mascarpone if necessary, then stir it into the egg yolk mixture. Beat until smooth.

4 In a separate bowl, mix the coffee, cocoa and liqueur. Break up the biscuits roughly, then stir them into the mixture.

5 Place the chocolate cups on individual plates. Divide half the biscuit mixture among them, then spoon over half the mascarpone mixture.

6 Spoon over the remaining biscuit mixture (including any free liquid), top with the rest of the mascarpone mixture and dust lightly with cocoa powder. Chill for about 30 minutes before serving.

CHOCOLATE CONES WITH APRICOT SAUCE

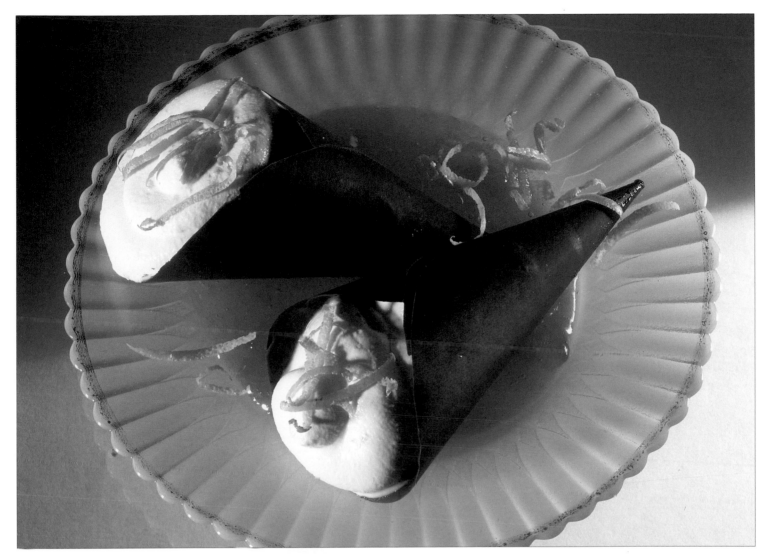

SERVES 6

*250g/9oz plain dark chocolate, chopped into
small pieces*
350g/12oz/1½ cups ricotta cheese
45ml/3 tbsp double cream
30ml/2 tbsp brandy
30ml/2 tbsp icing sugar
finely grated rind of 1 lemon
pared strips of lemon rind, to decorate

FOR THE SAUCE

175g/6oz/⅔ cup apricot jam
45ml/3 tbsp lemon juice

1 Cut twelve 10 cm/4 in double
thickness rounds from non-stick baking
paper and shape each into a cone. Secure
with masking tape.

2 Melt the chocolate over a saucepan of
simmering water. Cool slightly, then
spoon a little into each cone, swirling and
brushing it to coat the paper evenly.

3 Support each cone point downwards in
a cup or glass held on its side, to keep it
level. Leave in a cool place until the cones
are completely set. Unless it is a very hot
day, do not put the cones in the fridge, as
this may mar their appearance.

4 Make the sauce. Combine the apricot
jam and lemon juice in a small saucepan.
Melt over a gentle heat, stirring
occasionally, then press through a sieve
into a small bowl. Set aside to cool.

5 Beat the ricotta cheese in a bowl until
softened, then beat in the cream, brandy
and icing sugar. Stir in the lemon rind.
Spoon the mixture into a piping bag. Fill
the cones, then carefully peel off the non-
stick baking paper.

6 Spoon a pool of apricot sauce on to six
dessert plates. Arrange the cones in pairs
on the plates. Decorate with a scattering
of pared lemon rind strips and serve
immediately.

DEVILISH CHOCOLATE ROULADE

SERVES 6–8

*175g/6oz plain dark chocolate, chopped into
small pieces*
4 eggs, separated
115g/4oz/½ cup caster sugar
cocoa powder for dusting
chocolate-dipped strawberries, to decorate

FOR THE FILLING

*225g/8oz plain chocolate, chopped into
small pieces*
45ml/3 tbsp brandy
2 eggs, separated
250g/9oz/generous 1 cup mascarpone cheese

1 Preheat oven to 180°C/350°F/Gas 4.
Grease a 33 × 23 cm/13 × 9 in Swiss roll
tin and line with non-stick baking paper.
Melt the chocolate.

2 Whisk the egg yolks and sugar in a bowl
until pale and thick, then stir in the
melted chocolate. Place the egg whites in
a clean, grease-free bowl. Whisk them to
soft peaks, then fold lightly and evenly
into the egg and chocolate mixture.

3 Scrape into the tin and spread to the
corners. Bake for 15-20 minutes, until
well risen and firm to the touch. Dust a
sheet of non-stick baking paper with
cocoa powder. Turn the sponge out on
the paper, cover with a clean dish towel
and leave to cool.

4 Make the filling. Melt the chocolate
with the brandy in a heatproof bowl over
a saucepan of simmering water. Remove
from the heat. Beat the egg yolks
together, then beat into the chocolate
mixture. In a separate bowl whisk the
whites to soft peaks, then fold them
lightly and evenly into the filling.

5 Uncover the roulade, remove the lining
paper and spread with the mascarpone.
Spread the chocolate mixture over the
top, then roll up carefully from a long
side to enclose the filling. Transfer to a
serving plate with the join underneath,
top with fresh chocolate-dipped
strawberries and chill before serving.

COOK'S TIP

Chocolate-dipped strawberries make a
marvellous edible decoration for cakes
and desserts. Break plain, milk or
white chocolate into small pieces and
place in a small deep heatproof bowl
over a saucepan of barely simmering
water. While the chocolate melts, line
a baking sheet with non-stick baking
paper and set it aside.
Stir the melted chocolate until it is
completely smooth. Holding a
strawberry by its stalk or stalk end,
dip it partially or fully into the melted
chocolate, allowing any excess
chocolate to drip back into the bowl,
then place the fruit on the paper-lined
baking sheet. Repeat with the rest of
the fruit. Leave until the chocolate has
set. Use on the same day.
The same technique can be applied to
other relatively firm fruits, such as
cherries and orange segments.

CHOCOLATE MANDARIN TRIFLE

SERVES 6–8

4 trifle sponges
14 amaretti biscuits
60ml/4 tbsp Amaretto di Saronno or
sweet sherry
8 mandarin oranges
FOR THE CUSTARD
200g/7oz plain chocolate, chopped into
small pieces
30ml/2 tbsp cornflour or custard powder
30ml/2 tbsp caster sugar
2 egg yolks
200ml/7fl oz/scant 1 cup milk
250g/9oz/generous 1 cup mascarpone cheese
FOR THE TOPPING
250g/9oz/generous 1 cup fromage frais
chocolate shapes
mandarin slices or segments

1 Break up the trifle sponges and place them in a large glass serving dish. Crumble the amaretti biscuits over and then sprinkle with Amaretto or sherry.

2 Squeeze the juice from 2 mandarins and sprinkle into the dish. Segment the rest and put in the dish.

3 Make the custard. Melt the chocolate. In a heatproof bowl, mix the cornflour or custard powder, caster sugar and egg yolks to a smooth paste.

4 Heat the milk in a small saucepan until almost boiling, then pour on to the egg yolk mixture, stirring constantly. Return to the clean pan and stir over a low heat until the custard has thickened slightly and is smooth.

5 Stir in the mascarpone until melted, then mix in the melted chocolate. Spread over the sponge and biscuit, cool, then chill.

6 To serve, spread the fromage frais over the custard, then decorate with chocolate shapes and mandarin slices or segments.

COOK'S TIP
You can use canned mandarin oranges, if you prefer. Spoon about 30ml/2 tbsp of the juice over the sponge and biscuit mixture.

CHOCOLATE PROFITEROLES

4 Beat 1 egg in a small bowl and set aside. Add the whole eggs, one at a time, to the flour mixture, beating well after each addition. Beat in just enough of the beaten egg to make a smooth, shiny dough. It should pull away and fall slowly when dropped from a spoon.

5 Using a tablespoon, ease the dough in 12 mounds on to the prepared baking sheet. Bake for 25–30 minutes, until the puffs are golden brown.

6 Remove the puffs from the oven and cut a small slit in the side of each of them to release the steam. Return the puffs to the oven, turn off the heat and leave them to dry out, with the oven door open.

7 Remove the ice cream from the freezer and allow it to soften for about 10 minutes. Split the profiteroles in half and put a small scoop of ice cream in each. Arrange on a serving platter or divide among individual plates. Pour the sauce over the profiteroles and serve at once.

SERVES 4–6
110g / 3¾oz / scant 1 cup plain flour
1.5ml / ¼ tsp salt
pinch of freshly grated nutmeg
175ml / 6fl oz / ¾ cup water
75g / 3oz / 6 tbsp unsalted butter, cut into 6 equal pieces
3 eggs
750ml / 1¼ pints / 3 cups vanilla ice cream

FOR THE CHOCOLATE SAUCE
275g / 10oz plain chocolate, chopped into small pieces
120ml / 4fl oz / ½ cup warm water

1 Preheat oven to 200°C/400°F/Gas 6. Grease a baking sheet. Sift the flour, salt and nutmeg on to a sheet of greaseproof paper or foil.

2 Make the sauce. Melt the chocolate with the water in a heatproof bowl placed over a saucepan of barely simmering water. Stir until smooth. Keep warm until ready to serve, or reheat when required.

3 In a medium saucepan, bring the water and butter to the boil. Remove from the heat and add the dry ingredients all at once, funnelling them in from the paper or foil. Beat with a wooden spoon for about 1 minute until well blended and the mixture starts to pull away from the pan, then set the pan over a low heat and cook the mixture for about 2 minutes, beating constantly. Remove from the heat.

VARIATION
Fill the profiteroles with whipped cream, if you prefer. Spoon the cream into a piping bag and fill the slit puffs, or sandwich the halved puffs with the cream.

CHOCOLATE MINT ICE CREAM PIE

SERVES 8

75g/3 oz plain chocolate chips
40g/1½oz butter or margarine
50g/2oz crisped rice cereal
1 litre/1¾ pints/4 cups mint-chocolate-chip
ice cream
chocolate curls, to decorate

1 Line a 23 cm/9 in pie tin with foil. Place a round of greaseproof paper over the foil in the bottom of the tin.
2 In a heatproof bowl set over a saucepan of simmering water melt the chocolate chips with the butter or margarine.
3 Remove the bowl from the heat and gently stir in the cereal, a little at a time.

4 Press the chocolate-cereal mixture evenly over the base and up the sides of the prepared tin, forming a 1 cm/½ in rim. Chill until completely hard.
5 Carefully remove the cereal base from the tin and peel off the foil and paper. Return the base to the pie tin.

6 Remove the ice cream from the freezer and allow it to soften for 10 minutes.

7 Spread the ice cream evenly in the biscuit case crust. Freeze until firm.
8 Scatter the chocolate curls over the ice cream just before serving.

MANGO AND CHOCOLATE CREME BRULEE

SERVES 6

2 ripe mangoes, peeled, stoned and chopped
300ml / ½ pint / 1¼ cups double cream
300ml / ½ pint / 1¼ cups crème fraîche
1 vanilla pod
115g / 4oz plain dark chocolate, chopped into
small pieces
4 egg yolks
15ml / 1 tbsp clear honey
90ml / 6 tbsp demerara sugar, for the topping

<u>1</u> Divide the mangoes among six flameproof dishes set on a baking sheet.
<u>2</u> Mix the cream, crème fraîche and vanilla pod in a large heatproof bowl. Place the bowl over a pan of barely simmering water.

<u>3</u> Heat the cream mixture for 10 minutes. Do not let the bowl touch the water or the cream may overheat. Remove the vanilla pod and stir in the chocolate, a few pieces at a time, until melted. When smooth, remove the bowl, but leave the pan of water over the heat.

<u>4</u> Whisk the egg yolks and clear honey in a second heatproof bowl, then gradually pour in the chocolate cream, whisking constantly. Place over the pan of simmering water and stir constantly until the chocolate custard thickens enough to coat the back of a wooden spoon.
<u>5</u> Remove from the heat and spoon the custard over the mangoes. Cool, then chill in the fridge until set.
<u>6</u> Preheat the grill to high. Sprinkle 15ml / 1 tbsp demerara sugar evenly over each dessert and spray lightly with a little water. Grill briefly, as close to the heat as possible, until the sugar melts and caramelizes. Chill again before serving the desserts.

WHITE CHOCOLATE PARFAIT

SERVES 10

225g/8oz white chocolate, chopped into
small pieces
600ml/1 pint/2½ cups whipping cream
120ml/4fl oz/½ cup milk
10 egg yolks
15ml/1 tbsp caster sugar
40g/1½oz/½ cup desiccated coconut
120ml/4fl oz/½ cup canned sweetened
coconut milk
150g/5oz/1¼ cups unsalted macadamia nuts
curls of fresh coconut, to decorate

FOR THE CHOCOLATE ICING

225g/8oz plain chocolate, chopped into
small pieces
75g/3oz/6 tbsp butter
20ml/generous 1 tbsp golden syrup
175ml/6fl oz/¾ cup whipping cream

1 Carefully line the base and sides of a 1.4 litre/2⅓ pint/6 cup terrine mould or loaf tin with clear film.

2 Melt the chopped white chocolate with 50ml/2fl oz/¼ cup of the cream in the top of a double boiler or a heatproof bowl set over a saucepan of simmering water. Stir continually until the mixture is smooth. Set aside.

3 Put the milk in a pan. Add 250ml/8fl oz/1 cup of the remaining cream and bring to boiling point over a medium heat stirring constantly.

4 Meanwhile, whisk the egg yolks and caster sugar together in a large bowl, until thick and pale.

5 Add the hot cream mixture to the yolks, whisking constantly. Pour back into the saucepan and cook over a low heat for 2–3 minutes, until thickened. Stir constantly and do not boil. Remove the pan from the heat.

6 Add the melted chocolate, desiccated coconut and coconut milk, then stir well and leave to cool. Whip the remaining cream in a bowl until thick, then fold into the chocolate and coconut mixture.

7 Put 475ml/16fl oz/2 cups of the parfait mixture in the prepared mould or tin and spread evenly. Cover and freeze for about 2 hours, until just firm. Cover the remaining mixture and chill.

VARIATION

White Chocolate and Ginger Parfait: Use sliced stem ginger instead of macadamia nuts for the central layer of the parfait, and substitute syrup from the jar of ginger for the golden syrup in the icing. Leave out the coconut, if you prefer, and use sweetened condensed milk instead of the coconut milk.

8 Scatter the macadamia nuts evenly over the frozen parfait. Spoon in the remaining parfait mixture and level the surface. Cover the terrine and freeze for 6–8 hours or overnight, until the parfait is firm.

9 To make the icing, melt the chocolate with the butter and syrup in the top of a double boiler set over hot water. Stir occasionally.

10 Heat the cream in a saucepan, until just simmering, then stir into the chocolate mixture. Remove the pan from the heat and leave the mixture to cool until lukewarm.

11 To turn out the parfait, wrap the terrine or tin in a hot towel and set it upside down on a plate. Lift off the terrine or tin, then peel off the clear film. Place the parfait on a rack over a baking sheet and pour the icing evenly over the top. Working quickly, smooth the icing down the sides with a palette knife. Leave to set slightly, then transfer to a freezer-proof plate and freeze for 3–4 hours more.

12 Remove from the freezer about 15 minutes before serving, to allow the ice cream to soften slightly. When ready to serve, cut into slices, using a knife dipped in hot water between each slice. Serve, decorated with coconut curls.

CHOCOLATE ICE CREAM

SERVES 4–6

750ml / 1¼ pints / 3 cups milk
10 cm / 4 in piece of vanilla pod
4 egg yolks
115g / 4oz / ½ cup granulated sugar
225g / 8oz plain chocolate, chopped into small pieces

<u>1</u> Heat the milk with the vanilla pod in a small saucepan. Remove from the heat as soon as small bubbles start to form on the surface. Do not let it boil. Strain the milk into a jug and set aside.

<u>2</u> Using a wire whisk or hand-held electric mixer, beat the egg yolks in a bowl. Gradually whisk in the sugar and continue to whisk until the mixture is pale and thick. Slowly add the milk to the egg mixture, whisking after each addition. When all the milk has been added, pour the mixture into a heatproof bowl.

<u>3</u> Place the heatproof bowl over a saucepan of simmering water and add the chocolate. Stir over a low heat until the chocolate melts, then raise the heat slightly and continue to stir the chocolate-flavoured custard until it thickens enough to coat the back of a wooden spoon lightly. Remove the custard from the heat, pour into a bowl and allow to cool, stirring occasionally to prevent skin forming on the surface.

<u>4</u> Freeze the chocolate mixture in an ice-cream maker, following the manufacturer's instructions, or pour it into a suitable container for freezing. Freeze for about 3 hours, or until set. Remove from the container and chop roughly into 7.5 cm / 3 in pieces. Place in a food processor and chop until smooth. Return to the freezer container and freeze again. Repeat two or three times, until the ice cream is smooth and creamy.

CHOCOLATE FLAKE ICE CREAM

SERVES 6
300ml / ½ pint / 1¼ cups whipping cream,
chilled
90ml / 6 tbsp Greek-style yogurt
75–90ml / 5–6 tbsp caster sugar
few drops of vanilla essence
150g / 5oz / 10 tbsp flaked or roughly grated
chocolate

COOK'S TIPS
Transfer the ice cream from the freezer to the fridge about 15 minutes before serving, so that it softens, and so that the full flavour can be appreciated.
Use a metal scoop to serve the ice cream, dipping the scoop briefly in warm water between servings. If the ice cream has been made in a loaf tin, simply slice it.

1 Have ready an ice-cream maker, or use a 600 900ml / 1–1½ pint / 2½–3¾ cup freezer-proof container, preferably with a lid. Prepare a place in the freezer so you can easily reach it. If necessary, turn the freezer to the coldest setting.

2 Softly whip the cream in a large bowl then fold in the yogurt, sugar, vanilla essence and chocolate. Stir gently to mix thoroughly, and then transfer to the ice-cream maker or freezer container.

3 Smooth the surface of the ice cream, then cover and freeze. Gently stir with a fork every 30 minutes for up to 4 hours until the ice cream is too hard to stir. If using an ice-cream maker, follow the manufacturer's instructions.

CHOCOLATE FUDGE SUNDAES

SERVES 4

4 scoops each vanilla and coffee ice cream
2 small ripe bananas
whipped cream
toasted flaked almonds

FOR THE SAUCE

50g/2oz/⅓ cup soft light brown sugar
120ml/4fl oz/½ cup golden syrup
45ml/3 tbsp strong black coffee
5ml/1 tsp ground cinnamon
150g/5oz plain chocolate, chopped into
small pieces
75ml/3fl oz/5 tbsp whipping cream
45ml/3 tbsp coffee-flavoured liqueur
(optional)

1 Make the sauce. Place the sugar, syrup, coffee and cinnamon in a heavy-based saucepan. Bring to the boil, then boil for about 5 minutes, stirring the mixture constantly.

2 Turn off the heat and stir in the chocolate. When the chocolate has melted and the mixture is smooth, stir in the cream and the liqueur, if using. Leave the sauce to cool slightly. If made ahead, reheat the sauce gently until just warm.

3 Fill four glasses with a scoop each of vanilla and coffee ice cream.

4 Peel the bananas and slice them thinly. Scatter the sliced bananas over the ice cream. Pour the warm fudge sauce over the bananas, then top each sundae with a generous swirl of whipped cream. Sprinkle the sundaes with toasted almonds and serve at once.

ROCKY ROAD ICE CREAM

SERVES 6

*115g / 4oz plain chocolate, chopped into
small pieces
150ml / ¼ pint / ⅔ cup milk
300ml / ½ pint / 1¼ cups double cream
115g / 4oz / 2 cups marshmallows, chopped
115g / 4oz / ½ cup glacé cherries, chopped
50g / 2oz / ½ cup crumbled shortbread biscuits
30ml / 2 tbsp chopped walnuts*

1 Melt the chocolate in the milk in a saucepan over a gentle heat, stirring from time to time. Pour into a bowl and leave to cool completely.

2 Whip the cream in a separate bowl until it just holds its shape. Beat in the chocolate mixture, a little at a time, until the mixture is smooth and creamy.

3 Tip the mixture into an ice-cream maker and, following the manufacturer's instructions, churn until almost frozen. Alternatively, pour into a container suitable for use in the freezer, freeze until ice crystals form around the edges, then whisk with a strong hand whisk or hand-held electric mixer until smooth.

4 Stir the marshmallows, glacé cherries, crushed biscuits and nuts into the iced mixture, then return to the freezer container and freeze until firm.

5 Allow the ice cream to soften at room temperature for 15–20 minutes before serving in scoops. Add a wafer and chocolate sauce to each portion, if desired.

ICED CHOCOLATE NUT GATEAU

SERVES 6–8

75g / 3oz / ¾ cup shelled hazelnuts
about 32 sponge fingers
150ml / ¼ pint / ⅔ cup cold strong black coffee
30ml / 2 tbsp brandy
475ml / 16fl oz / 2 cups double cream
75g / 3oz / generous ½ cup icing sugar, sifted
150g / 5oz plain chocolate, chopped into
small pieces
icing sugar and cocoa powder, for dusting

1 Preheat oven to 200°C / 400°F / Gas 6. Spread out the hazelnuts on a baking sheet and toast them in the oven for 5 minutes until golden. Tip the nuts on to a clean dish towel and rub off the skins while still warm. Cool, then chop finely.

2 Line a 1.2 litre / 2 pint / 5 cup loaf tin with clear film and cut the sponge fingers to fit the base and sides. Reserve the remaining biscuits. Mix the coffee with the brandy in a shallow dish. Dip the sponge fingers briefly into the coffee mixture and return to the tin, sugary side down to fit neatly.

3 Whip the cream with the icing sugar until it holds soft peaks. Fold half the chopped chocolate into the cream with the hazelnuts. Use a gentle figure-of-eight action to distribute the chocolate and nuts evenly.

4 Melt the remaining chocolate in a bowl set over a pan of barely simmering water. Cool, then fold into the cream mixture. Spoon into the tin.

5 Moisten the remaining biscuits in the coffee mixture, be careful not to soak the biscuits, as they will collapse. Lay the coffee-moistened biscuits over the filling. Wrap and freeze until firm.

6 To serve, remove from the freezer 30 minutes before serving to allow the ice cream to soften slightly. Turn out on to a serving plate and dust with icing sugar and cocoa.

ICED CHOCOLATE AND MANDARIN GATEAU

Dip the sponge fingers in a mixture of strong black coffee and mandarin or orange liqueur. Omit the hazelnuts from the cream filling. About 30 minutes before serving, remove the frozen gâteau from the tin and place it on a serving plate. Cover with whipped cream flavoured with mandarin or orange liqueur. Pipe more whipped cream around the base of the gâteau. Decorate with plain or chocolate-dipped mandarin or orange segments.

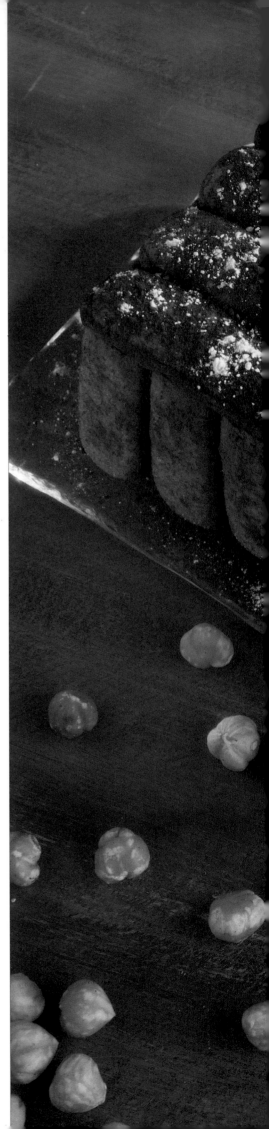

CHOCOLATE BISCUITS AND COOKIES

CHOC-CHIP NUT BISCUITS

MAKES 36

115g/4oz/1 cup plain flour
5ml/1 tsp baking powder
5ml/1 tsp salt
75g/3oz/6 tbsp butter or margarine
115g/4oz/1 cup caster sugar
50g/2oz/⅓ cup soft light brown sugar
1 egg
5ml/1 tsp vanilla essence
115g/4oz/⅔ cup plain chocolate chips
50g/2oz/½ cup hazelnuts, chopped

1 Preheat oven to 180°C/350°F/Gas 4. Grease 2–3 baking sheets. Sift the flour, baking powder and salt into a small bowl. Set the bowl aside.

2 With a hand-held electric mixer, cream the butter or margarine and sugars together. Beat in the egg and vanilla essence. Add the flour mixture and beat well on low speed.

3 Stir in the chocolate chips and half of the hazelnuts. Drop teaspoonfuls of the mixture on to the prepared baking sheets, to form 2 cm/¾ in mounds. Space the biscuits about 5 cm/2 in apart to allow room for spreading.

4 Flatten each biscuit lightly with a wet fork. Sprinkle the remaining hazelnuts on top of the biscuits and press lightly into the surface. Bake for 10–12 minutes, until golden brown. Transfer the biscuits to a wire rack and allow to cool.

CHOC-CHIP OAT BISCUITS

MAKES 60

115g/4oz/1 cup plain flour
2.5ml/½ tsp bicarbonate of soda
1.5ml/¼ tsp baking powder
1.5ml/¼ tsp salt
115g/4oz/1 cup butter or margarine, softened
115g/4oz/1 cup caster sugar
75g/3oz/½ cup light brown sugar
1 egg
1.5ml/¼ tsp vanilla essence
75g/3oz/scant 1 cup rolled oats
175g/6oz/1 cup plain chocolate chips

1 Preheat oven to 180°C/350°F/Gas 4. Grease 3–4 baking sheets. Sift the flour, bicarbonate of soda, baking powder and salt into a mixing bowl. Set the bowl aside.

2 With a hand-held electric mixer, cream the butter or margarine and sugars together in a bowl. Add the egg and vanilla essence and beat until light and fluffy.

3 Add the flour mixture and beat on low speed until thoroughly blended. Stir in the rolled oats and chocolate chips, mixing well with a wooden spoon. The dough should be crumbly.

4 Drop heaped teaspoonfuls on to the prepared baking sheets, spacing the dough about 2.5 cm/1 in apart. Bake for about 15 minutes until just firm around the edge but still soft to the touch in the centre. With a slotted spatula, transfer the biscuits to a wire rack and allow them to cool.

CHOCOLATE-DIPPED HAZELNUT CRESCENTS

MAKES ABOUT 35
275g/10oz/2 cups plain flour
pinch of salt
225g/8oz/1 cup unsalted butter, softened
75g/3oz/6 tbsp caster sugar
15ml/1 tbsp hazelnut-flavoured liqueur
or water
5ml/1 tsp vanilla essence
75g/3oz plain chocolate, chopped into
small pieces
50g/2oz/½ cup hazelnuts, toasted and
finely chopped
icing sugar, for dusting
350g/12oz plain chocolate, melted, for
dipping

1 Preheat oven to 160°C/325°F/Gas 3. Grease two large baking sheets. Sift the flour and salt into a bowl. In a separate bowl, beat the butter until creamy. Add the sugar and beat until fluffy, then beat in the hazelnut liqueur or water and the vanilla essence. Gently stir in the flour mixture, then the chocolate and hazelnuts.

2 With floured hands, shape the dough into 5 x 1 cm/2 x ½ in crescent shapes. Place on the baking sheets, 5 cm/2 in apart. Bake for 20–25 minutes until the edges are set and the biscuits slightly golden. Remove the biscuits from the oven and cool on the baking sheets for 10 minutes, then transfer the biscuits to wire racks to cool completely.

3 Have the melted chocolate ready in a small bowl. Dust the biscuits lightly with icing sugar. Using a pair of kitchen tongs or your fingers, dip half of each crescent into the melted chocolate. Place the crescents on a non-stick baking sheet until the chocolate has set.

CHUNKY DOUBLE CHOCOLATE COOKIES

MAKES 18–20

115g/4oz/½ cup unsalted butter, softened
115g/4oz/⅔ cup light muscovado sugar
1 egg
5ml/1 tsp vanilla essence
150g/5oz/1¼ cups self-raising flour
75g/3oz/¾ cup porridge oats
115g/4oz plain chocolate, roughly chopped
115g/4oz white chocolate, roughly chopped

DOUBLE-CHOC ALMOND COOKIES:
Instead of the porridge oats, use 75g/3oz/¾ cup ground almonds. Omit the chopped chocolate and use 175g/6oz/1 cup chocolate chips instead. Top each heap of cake mixture with half a glacé cherry before baking.

<u>1</u> Preheat oven to 190°C/375°F/Gas 5. Lightly grease two baking sheets. Cream the butter with the sugar in a bowl until pale and fluffy. Add the egg and vanilla essence and beat well.
<u>2</u> Sift the flour over the mixture and fold in lightly with a metal spoon, then add the oats and chopped plain and white chocolate and stir until evenly mixed.

<u>3</u> Place small spoonfuls of the mixture in 18–20 rocky heaps on the baking sheets, leaving space for spreading.
<u>4</u> Bake for 12–15 minutes or until the biscuits are beginning to turn pale golden. Cool for 2–3 minutes on the baking sheets, then lift on to wire racks. The biscuits will be soft when freshly baked but will harden on cooling.

CHOCOLATE MARZIPAN COOKIES

MAKES ABOUT 36

*200g / 7oz / scant 1 cup unsalted butter,
softened*
*200g / 7oz / generous 1 cup light muscovado
sugar*
1 egg, beaten
300g / 11oz / 2¾ cups plain flour
60ml / 4 tbsp cocoa powder
200g / 7oz white almond paste
*115g / 4oz white chocolate, chopped into
small pieces*

1 Preheat oven to 190°C/375°F/Gas 5.
Lightly grease two large baking sheets.
Using a hand-held electric mixer, cream
the butter with the sugar in a mixing
bowl until pale and fluffy. Add the egg
and beat well.

2 Sift the flour and cocoa over the
mixture. Stir in with a wooden spoon
until all the flour mixture has been
smoothly incorporated, then use clean
hands to press the mixture together to
make a fairly soft dough.

3 Using a rolling pin and keeping your
touch light, roll out about half the dough
on a lightly floured surface to a thickness
of about 5 mm / ¼ in. Using a 5 cm / 2 in
plain or fluted biscuit cutter, cut out 36
rounds, re-rolling the dough as required.
Wrap the remaining dough in clear film
and set it aside.

4 Cut the almond paste into 36 equal
pieces. Roll into balls, flatten slightly and
place one on each round of dough. Roll
out the remaining dough, cut out more
rounds, then place on top of the almond
paste. Press the dough edges to seal.

5 Bake for 10–12 minutes, or until the
cookies have risen well and are beginning
to crack on the surface. Cool on the
baking sheet for about 2–3 minutes, then
finish cooling on a wire rack.

6 Melt the white chocolate, then either
drizzle it over the biscuits to decorate, or
spoon into a paper piping bag and quickly
pipe a design on to the biscuits.

VARIATION
Use glacé icing instead of melted
white chocolate to decorate the
cookies, if you prefer.

BLACK AND WHITE GINGER FLORENTINES

MAKES ABOUT 30

120ml/4fl oz/½ cup double cream
50g/2oz/¼ cup butter
50g/2oz/¼ cup granulated sugar
30ml/2 tbsp honey
150g/5oz/1¼ cups flaked almonds
40g/1½oz/6 tbsp plain flour
2.5ml/½ tsp ground ginger
50g/2oz/⅓ cup diced candied orange peel
75g/3oz/½ cup diced stem ginger
50g/2oz plain chocolate, chopped into
small pieces
150g/5oz bittersweet chocolate, chopped into
small pieces
150g/5oz fine quality white chocolate,
chopped into small pieces

1 Preheat oven to 180°C/350°F/Gas 4. Lightly grease two large baking sheets. In a saucepan over a medium heat, stir the cream, butter, sugar and honey until the sugar dissolves. Bring the mixture to the boil, stirring constantly. Remove from the heat and stir in the almonds, flour and ground ginger. Stir in the candied peel, ginger and plain chocolate.

2 Drop teaspoons of the mixture on to the baking sheets at least 7.5 cm/3 in apart. Spread each round as thinly as possible with the back of the spoon.

3 Bake for 8–10 minutes or until the edges are golden brown and the biscuits are bubbling. Do not under-bake or they will be sticky, but be careful not to over-bake as they burn easily. Continue baking in batches. If you wish, use a 7.5 cm/3 in biscuit cutter to neaten the edges of the florentines while they are still on the baking sheet.

4 Allow the biscuits to cool on the baking sheets for 10 minutes, until they are firm enough to move. Using a metal palette knife, carefully lift the biscuits on to a wire rack to cool completely.

5 Melt the bittersweet chocolate in a heatproof bowl over barely simmering water. Cool slightly. Put the white chocolate in a separate bowl and melt in the same way, stirring frequently. Remove and cool for about 5 minutes, stirring occasionally.

6 Using a small metal palette knife, spread half the florentines with the bittersweet chocolate and half with the melted white chocolate. Place on a wire rack, chocolate side up. Chill for 10–15 minutes to set completely.

CHEWY CHOCOLATE BISCUITS
MAKES 18

4 egg whites
350g/12oz/2½ cups icing sugar
115g/4oz/1 cup cocoa powder
30ml/2 tbsp plain flour
5ml/1 tsp instant coffee
15ml/1 tbsp water
115g/4oz/1 cup walnuts, finely chopped

1 Preheat oven to 180°C/350°F/Gas 4. Line two baking sheets with non-stick baking paper.
2 With a hand-held electric mixer, beat the egg whites in a bowl until frothy.
3 Sift the icing sugar, cocoa powder, flour and coffee into the whites. Add the water and continue beating on low speed to blend, then on high speed for a few minutes until the mixture thickens. With a rubber spatula, fold in the walnuts.
4 Place generous spoonfuls of the mixture 2.5 cm/1 in apart on the prepared baking sheets. Bake for 12–15 minutes, or until firm and cracked on top but soft on the inside. With a metal spatula, transfer the biscuits to a wire rack to cool.

CHOCOLATE CRACKLE-TOPS

MAKES ABOUT 38
200g/7oz bittersweet or plain chocolate,
chopped into small pieces
90g/3½oz/7 tbsp unsalted butter
115g/4oz/½ cup caster sugar
3 eggs
5ml/1 tsp vanilla essence
200g/7oz/1¾ cups plain flour
25g/1oz/¼ cup cocoa powder
2.5ml/½ tsp baking powder
pinch of salt
175g/6oz/1½ cups icing sugar, for coating

1 Grease two or more large baking sheets. In a heavy-based saucepan over a low heat, melt the chocolate and butter until smooth, stirring frequently. Remove from the heat. Stir in the sugar until dissolved. Add the eggs, one at a time, beating well after each addition. Stir in the vanilla essence.

2 Sift the flour, cocoa, baking powder and salt into a bowl. Gradually stir into the chocolate mixture in batches to make a soft dough. Cover in clear film and chill for at least 1 hour until the dough is firm enough to hold its shape.

3 Preheat oven to 160°C/325°F/Gas 3. Place the icing sugar in a small, deep bowl. Using a small ice cream scoop or round teaspoon, scoop the dough into small balls and roll between your palms.

4 Drop the balls, one at a time, into the icing sugar and roll until heavily coated. Remove each ball with a slotted spoon and tap the spoon against the bowl to remove excess sugar. Place the balls on the baking sheets, about 4 cm/1½ in apart.

5 Bake the biscuits for 10–15 minutes or until the top of each feels slightly firm when touched with a fingertip. Leave for 2–3 minutes, until just set. Transfer to wire racks and leave to cool completely.

CHUNKY CHOCOLATE DROPS

MAKES ABOUT 18

175g/6oz bittersweet or plain chocolate,
chopped into small pieces
115g/4oz/½ cup unsalted butter, diced
2 eggs
115g/4oz/½ cup granulated sugar
50g/2oz/⅓ cup light brown sugar
40g/1½oz/6 tbsp plain flour
25g/1oz/¼ cup cocoa powder
5ml/1 tsp baking powder
10ml/2 tsp vanilla essence
pinch of salt
115g/4oz/1 cup pecan nuts, toasted and
coarsely chopped
175g/6oz/1 cup plain chocolate chips
115g/4oz fine quality white chocolate,
chopped into small pieces
115g/4oz fine quality milk chocolate,
chopped into small pieces

1 Preheat oven to 160°C/325°F/Gas 3. Grease two large baking sheets. In a medium saucepan over a low heat, melt the chocolate and butter until smooth, stirring frequently. Remove from the heat and leave to cool slightly.

2 In a large mixing bowl, beat the eggs and sugars until pale and creamy. Gradually pour in the melted chocolate mixture, beating well. Beat in the flour, cocoa, baking powder and vanilla essence. Stir in the remaining ingredients.

3 Drop heaped tablespoons of the mixture on to the baking sheets, 10 cm/ 4 in apart. Flatten each to a 7.5 cm/ 3 in round. (You will only get 4–6 biscuits on each sheet.) Bake for 8–10 minutes until the tops are shiny and cracked and the edges look crisp. Do not over-bake or the biscuits will break when they are removed from the baking sheets.

4 Remove the baking sheets to wire racks to cool for 2 minutes, until the biscuits are just set, then carefully transfer them to the wire racks to cool completely. Bake the biscuits in batches, if necessary. Store in airtight containers.

CHOCOLATE AMARETTI

MAKES ABOUT 24

115g/4oz/1 cup blanched whole almonds
115g/4oz/½ cup caster sugar
15ml/1 tbsp cocoa powder
30ml/2 tbsp icing sugar
2 egg whites
pinch of cream of tartar
5ml/1 tsp almond essence
flaked almonds, to decorate

<u>1</u> Preheat oven to 180°C/350°F/Gas 4. Place the almonds on a small baking sheet and bake for 10–12 minutes, turning occasionally until golden brown. Cool to room temperature. Reduce the oven temperature to 160°C/325°F/Gas 3.

<u>2</u> Line a large baking sheet with non-stick baking paper. In a food processor, process the toasted almonds with half the caster sugar until the almonds are finely ground but not oily. Transfer the ground almonds to a bowl and stir in the cocoa powder and icing sugar. Set aside.

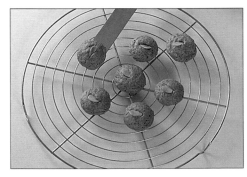

<u>3</u> In a medium mixing bowl, beat the egg whites and cream of tartar with a hand-held mixer, until stiff peaks form. Sprinkle in the remaining caster sugar about 15ml/1 tbsp at a time, beating well after each addition, and continue beating until the whites are glossy and stiff. Beat in the almond essence.

<u>4</u> Sprinkle over the almond-sugar mixture and gently fold into the beaten egg whites until just blended. Spoon the mixture into a large piping bag fitted with a plain 1 cm/½ in nozzle. Pipe 4 cm/1½ in rounds about 2.5 cm/1 in apart on the prepared baking sheet. Press a flaked almond into the centre of each biscuit.

<u>5</u> Bake the biscuits for 12–15 minutes or until they are crisp. Cool on the baking sheet for 10 minutes. With a metal palette knife, transfer the biscuits to wire racks to cool completely. When cool, store in an airtight jar or biscuit tin. Serve after a dinner party with coffee, or use in trifles.

CHOCOLATE KISSES

MAKES 24

75g/3oz dark plain chocolate, chopped into small pieces
75g/3oz white chocolate, chopped into small pieces
115g/4oz/½ cup butter, softened
115g/4oz/½ cup caster sugar
2 eggs
225g/8oz/2 cups plain flour
icing sugar, to decorate

1 Melt the plain and white chocolates in separate bowls and set both aside to cool.
2 Beat the butter and caster sugar together until pale and fluffy. Beat in the eggs, one at a time. Then sift in the flour and mix well.

3 Halve the creamed mixture and divide it between the two bowls of chocolate. Mix each chocolate in thoroughly so that each forms a dough. Knead the doughs until smooth, wrap them separately in clear film and chill for 1 hour. Preheat oven to 190°C/375°F/Gas 5.

4 Shape slightly rounded teaspoonfuls of both doughs roughly into balls. Roll the balls between your palms to neaten them. Arrange the balls on greased baking sheets and bake for 10–12 minutes. Dust liberally with sifted icing sugar and cool on a wire rack.

MOCHA VIENNESE SWIRLS

MAKES ABOUT 20

115g/4oz plain chocolate, chopped into
small pieces
200g/7oz/scant 1 cup unsalted butter,
softened
90ml/6 tbsp icing sugar
30ml/2 tbsp strong black coffee
200g/7oz/1¾ cups plain flour
50g/2oz/½ cup cornflour

TO DECORATE

about 20 blanched almonds
150g/5oz plain chocolate, chopped into
small pieces

1 Preheat oven to 190°C/375°F/Gas 5. Melt the chocolate in a bowl over barely simmering water. Cream the butter with the icing sugar in a bowl until smooth and pale. Beat in the melted chocolate, then the strong black coffee.

2 Sift the plain flour and cornflour over the mixture. Fold in lightly and evenly to make a soft biscuit dough.

3 Lightly grease two large baking sheets. Spoon the dough into a piping bag fitted with a large star nozzle. Pipe about 20 swirls on the baking sheets, allowing room for spreading. Keep the nozzle close to the sheet so that the swirls are flat.

4 Press an almond into the centre of each swirl. Bake for about 15 minutes or until the biscuits are firm and starting to brown. Cool for about 10 minutes on the baking sheets, then lift carefully on to a wire rack to cool completely.

5 When cool, melt the chocolate and dip the base of each swirl to coat. Place on a sheet of non-stick baking paper and leave to set completely.

CHOCOLATE MACAROONS

MAKES 24

50g/2oz plain chocolate, chopped into
small pieces
115g/4oz/1 cup blanched almonds
225g/8oz/1 cup granulated sugar
3 egg whites
2.5ml/½ tsp vanilla essence
1.5ml/¼ tsp almond essence
icing sugar, for dusting

1 Preheat oven to 160°C/325°F/Gas 3. Line two baking sheets with non-stick baking paper.

VARIATION

For Chocolate Pine Nut Macaroons, spread 50g/2oz/⅔ cup toasted pine nuts in a shallow dish. Press the balls of chocolate macaroon dough into the nuts to cover one side and bake as described, nut-side up.

2 Melt the chocolate in the top of a double boiler, or in a heatproof bowl placed over a saucepan of barely simmering water.

3 Grind the almonds finely in a food processor, blender or nut grinder. Transfer to a mixing bowl.

4 Add the sugar, egg whites, vanilla essence and almond essence and stir to blend. Stir in the chocolate. The mixture should just hold its shape. If it is too soft, chill it in the fridge for 15 minutes.

5 Use a teaspoon and your hands to shape the dough into walnut-size balls. Place on the baking sheets and flatten slightly. Brush each ball with a little water and sift over a thin layer of icing sugar. Bake for 10–12 minutes, until just firm. With a metal spatula, transfer to a wire rack to cool completely.

CHOCOLATE CINNAMON TUILES

3 In a separate bowl, mix together the cocoa and cinnamon. Stir into the larger quantity of mixture until well combined. Leaving room for spreading, drop spoonfuls of the chocolate-flavoured mixture on to the prepared baking sheets, then spread each gently with a palette knife to make a neat round.

4 Using a small spoon, drizzle the reserved plain mixture over the rounds, swirling it lightly to give a marbled effect.

5 Bake for 4–6 minutes, until just set. Using a palette knife, lift each biscuit and drape it over a rolling pin, to give a curved shape as it hardens. Allow the tuiles to set, then remove them and finish cooling on a wire rack. Serve on the same day.

MAKES 12

1 egg white
50g/2oz/¼ cup caster sugar
30ml/2 tbsp plain flour
40g/1½oz/3 tbsp butter, melted
15ml/1 tbsp cocoa powder
2.5m/½ tsp ground cinnamon

1 Preheat oven to 200°C/400°F/Gas 6. Lightly grease two large baking sheets. Whisk the egg white in a clean, grease-free bowl until it forms soft peaks. Gradually whisk in the sugar to make a smooth, glossy mixture.

2 Sift the flour over the meringue mixture and fold in evenly; try not to deflate the mixture. Stir in the butter. Transfer about 45ml/3 tbsp of the mixture to a small bowl and set it aside.

CHOCOLATE CUPS

Cream 150g/5oz/⅔ cup butter with 115g/4oz/½ cup caster sugar. Stir in 75g/3oz/1 cup porridge oats, 15ml/1 tbsp cocoa powder and 5ml/1 tsp vanilla essence. Roll to the size of golf balls and space well on greased baking sheets. Bake at 180°C/350°F/Gas 4 for 12–15 minutes. Cool slightly then drape over greased upturned glasses until cool and firm. Makes 8–10.

CHOCOLATE PRETZELS

MAKES 28

150g/5oz/1¼ cups plain flour
pinch of salt
25g/1oz/¼ cup cocoa powder
115g/4oz/½ cup butter, softened
115g/4oz/½ cup caster sugar
1 egg
1 egg white, lightly beaten, for glazing
sugar crystals, for sprinkling

1 Sift the plain flour, salt and cocoa powder into a bowl. Set aside. Grease two baking sheets.

2 With a hand-held electric mixer, cream the butter. Add the caster sugar and beat until fluffy. Beat in the egg. Stir in the dry ingredients. Gather the dough into a ball and chill for 1 hour.

3 Roll the dough into 28 small balls. Preheat the oven to 190°C/375°F/Gas 5. Roll each ball into a rope about 25 cm/ 10 in long. With each rope, form a loop with the two ends facing you. Twist the ends and fold back on to the circle, pressing in to make a pretzel shape. Place on the greased baking sheets.

4 Brush the pretzels with the egg white. Sprinkle sugar crystals over the tops and bake for 10–12 minutes until firm. Transfer to a wire rack to cool.

LITTLE CAKES, SLICES AND BARS

CHOCOLATE FAIRY CAKES

MAKES 24

*115g/4oz plain chocolate, chopped into
small pieces*
15ml/1 tbsp water
275g/10oz/2½ cups plain flour
5ml/1 tsp baking powder
2.5ml/½ tsp bicarbonate of soda
pinch of salt
300g/11oz/scant 1½ cups caster sugar
*175g/6oz/¾ cup butter or margarine, at
room temperature*
150ml/¼ pint/⅔ cup milk
5ml/1 tsp vanilla essence
3 eggs

FOR THE ICING

40g/1½ oz/3 tbsp butter or margarine
115g/4oz/1 cup icing sugar
2.5ml/½ tsp vanilla essence
15–30ml/1–2 tbsp milk

1 Preheat oven to 180°C/350°F/Gas 4.
Grease 24 bun tins, about 6.5 cm/2¾ in
in diameter and line with paper cases.
2 Make the icing. Soften the butter or
margarine. Place it in a bowl and stir in
the icing sugar, a little at a time. Add the
vanilla essence, then, a drop at a time,
beat in just enough milk to make a
creamy, spreadable mixture. Cover the
surface closely with clear film and set the
bowl aside.

3 Melt the chocolate with the water in a
heatproof bowl over simmering water.
Remove from the heat. Sift the flour,
baking powder, bicarbonate of soda, salt
and sugar into a large bowl. Add the
chocolate mixture, butter or margarine,
milk and vanilla essence.

4 With a hand-held electric mixer on
medium speed, beat the mixture until
smooth. Increase the speed to high and
beat for 2 minutes. Add the eggs, one at a
time, and beat for 1 minute after each
addition. Divide the mixture evenly
among the prepared bun tins.

5 Bake for 20–25 minutes or until a
skewer inserted into the centre of a cake
comes out clean. Cool in the tins for
10 minutes, then turn out to cool
completely on a wire rack. Spread the top
of each cake with the icing, swirling it
into a peak in the centre.

CHOCOLATE MINT-FILLED CUPCAKES

MAKES 12

225g / 8oz / 2 cups plain flour
5ml / 1 tsp bicarbonate of soda
pinch of salt
50g / 2oz / ½ cup cocoa powder
150g / 5oz / 10 tbsp unsalted butter, softened
350g / 12oz / 1⅔ cups caster sugar
3 eggs
5ml / 1 tsp peppermint essence
250ml / 8 fl oz / 1 cup milk

FOR THE MINT CREAM FILLING

300ml / ½ pint / 1¼ cups double cream or whipping cream
5ml / 1 tsp peppermint essence

FOR THE CHOCOLATE MINT GLAZE

175g / 6oz plain chocolate, chopped into small pieces
115g / 4oz / ½ cup unsalted butter
5ml / 1 tsp peppermint essence

1 Preheat oven to 180°C / 350°F / Gas 4. Line a 12-hole bun tin with paper cases, using the cases double if they are thin. Sift the flour, bicarbonate of soda, salt and cocoa powder into a bowl. Set aside.

2 In a large mixing bowl, beat the butter and sugar with a hand held electric mixer for about 3–5 minutes until light and creamy. Add the eggs, one at a time, beating well after each addition and adding a small amount of the flour mixture if the egg mixture shows signs of curdling. Beat in the peppermint essence until thoroughly mixed.

3 With the hand-held electric mixer on a low speed, beat in the flour-cocoa mixture alternately with the milk, until just blended. Spoon into the paper cases, filling them about three-quarters full.

4 Bake for 12–15 minutes, until a cake tester inserted in the centre of one of the cupcakes comes out clean.

5 Lift the cupcakes on to a wire rack to cool completely. When cool, carefully remove the paper cases.

6 Prepare the mint cream filling. In a small bowl, whip the cream and peppermint essence until stiff. Fit a small, plain nozzle into a piping bag and spoon in the flavoured cream. Gently press the nozzle into the bottom of one of the cupcakes. Squeeze gently, releasing about 15ml / 1 tbsp of the flavoured cream into the centre of the cake. Repeat with the remaining cupcakes, returning each one to the wire rack as it is filled.

7 Prepare the glaze. In a saucepan over a low heat, melt the chocolate and butter, stirring until smooth. Remove from heat and stir in the peppermint essence. Cool then spread on the top of each cake.

CHOCOLATE CREAM PUFFS

MAKES 12 LARGE CREAM PUFFS
115g/4oz/1 cup plain flour
30ml/2 tbsp cocoa powder
250ml/8fl oz/1 cup water
2.5ml/½ tsp salt
15ml/1 tbsp granulated sugar
115g/4oz/½ cup unsalted butter, diced
4 eggs
FOR THE CHOCOLATE PASTRY CREAM
450ml/¾ pint/2 cups milk
6 egg yolks
115g/4oz/½ cup granulated sugar
50g/2oz/½ cup plain flour
150g/5oz plain chocolate, chopped into small pieces
115ml/4fl oz/½ cup whipping cream
FOR THE CHOCOLATE GLAZE
300ml/½ pint/1¼ cups whipping cream
50g/2oz/¼ cup unsalted butter, diced
225g/8oz bittersweet or plain chocolate, chopped into small pieces
15ml/1 tbsp golden syrup
5ml/1 tsp vanilla essence

1 Preheat oven to 220°C/425°F/Gas 7. Lightly grease two large baking sheets. Sift the flour and cocoa powder into a bowl. In a saucepan over a medium heat, bring to the boil the water, salt, sugar and butter. Remove the pan from the heat and add the flour and cocoa mixture all at once, stirring vigorously until the mixture is smooth and leaves the sides of the pan clean.

2 Return the pan to the heat to cook the choux pastry for 1 minute, beating constantly. Remove from the heat.

3 With a hand-held electric mixer, beat in 4 of the eggs, one at a time, beating well after each addition, until each is well blended. The mixture should be thick and shiny and just fall from a spoon. Spoon the mixture into a large piping bag fitted with a plain nozzle. Pipe 12 mounds about 7.5 cm/3 in across at least 5 cm/2 in apart on the baking sheet.

4 Bake for 35–40 minutes until puffed and firm. Remove the puffs. Using a serrated knife, slice off and reserve the top third of each puff; return the opened puffs to the oven for 5–10 minutes to dry out. Remove to a wire rack to cool.

5 Prepare the pastry cream. Bring the milk to the boil in a small pan. In a bowl, heat the yolks and sugar until pale and thick. Stir in the flour. Slowly pour about 250ml/8fl oz/1 cup of the hot milk into the yolks, stirring constantly. Return the yolk mixture to the remaining milk in the pan and cook, stirring until the sauce boils for 1 minute. Remove from the heat and stir in the chocolate until smooth.

6 Strain into a bowl and cover closely with clear film. Cool to room temperature. In a bowl, whip the cream until stiff. Fold into the pastry cream.

7 Using a large piping bag, fill each puff bottom with pastry cream, then cover each puff with its top. Arrange the cream puffs on a large serving plate in a single layer or as a pile.

8 Make the glaze by heating the cream, butter, chocolate, syrup and vanilla essence in a medium saucepan over low heat until melted and smooth, stirring frequently. Cool for 20–30 minutes until slightly thickened. Pour a little glaze over each of the cream puffs to serve.

CHOCOLATE BUTTERSCOTCH BARS

MAKES 24

225g/8oz/2 cups plain flour
2.5ml/½ tsp baking powder
150g/5oz plain chocolate, chopped
115g/4oz/½ cup unsalted butter, diced
50g/2oz/⅓ cup light muscovado sugar
30ml/2 tbsp ground almonds

FOR THE TOPPING

175g/6oz/¾ cup unsalted butter, diced
115g/4oz/½ cup caster sugar
30ml/2 tbsp golden syrup
175ml/6fl oz/¾ cup condensed milk
150g/5oz/1¼ cups whole toasted hazelnuts
225g/8oz plain chocolate, chopped into small pieces

1 Preheat oven to 160°C/325°F/Gas 3. Grease a shallow 30 x 20 cm/12 x 8 in tin. Sift the flour and baking powder into a large bowl. Melt the chocolate in a bowl over a saucepan of simmering water.

2 Rub the butter into the flour until the mixture resembles coarse breadcrumbs, then stir in the sugar. Work in the melted chocolate and ground almonds to make a light biscuit dough.

3 Spread the dough roughly in the tin, then use a rubber spatula to press it down evenly into the sides and the corners. Prick the surface with a fork and bake for 25–30 minutes until firm. Leave to cool in the tin.

4 Make the topping. Heat the butter, sugar, golden syrup and condensed milk in a pan, stirring until the butter and sugar have melted. Simmer until golden, then stir in the hazelnuts.

5 Pour over the cooked base. Leave to set.

6 Melt the chocolate for the topping in a heatproof bowl over barely simmering water. Spread evenly over the butterscotch layer, then leave to set again before cutting into bars to serve.

CHOCOLATE WALNUT BARS

MAKES 24

50g / 2oz / ½ cup walnuts
50g / 2oz / ¼ cup caster sugar
115g / 4oz / 1 cup plain flour, sifted
75g / 3oz unsalted butter, cut into pieces

FOR THE TOPPING

25g / 1oz / 2 tbsp unsalted butter
75ml / 3fl oz / 5 tbsp water
25g / 1oz / ¼ cup cocoa powder
115g / 4oz / ½ cup caster sugar
5ml / 1 tsp vanilla essence
pinch of salt
2 eggs
icing sugar, for dusting

<u>1</u> Preheat oven to 180°C/350°F/Gas 4.
Grease the base and sides of a 20 cm/8 in
square baking tin.

<u>2</u> Grind the walnuts with 15–30ml/
1–2 tbsp of the sugar in a food processor,
blender or coffee grinder.
<u>3</u> In a bowl, combine the ground walnuts,
remaining sugar and flour. With your
fingertips, rub in the butter until the
mixture resembles coarse breadcrumbs.
Alternatively, process all the ingredients
in a food processor until the mixture
resembles coarse breadcrumbs.

<u>4</u> Pat the walnut mixture on to the base
of the prepared tin in an even layer. Bake
for 25 minutes.

<u>5</u> Meanwhile make the topping. Heat the
butter with the water in a saucepan over a
medium heat. When all the butter has
melted, gradually whisk in the cocoa
powder and caster sugar. Remove from
the heat, stir in the vanilla essence and
salt and set the mixture aside to cool for
5 minutes. Whisk in the eggs until
blended.

<u>6</u> Pour the topping over the baked crust,
return the baking tin to the oven and bake
for about 20 minutes or until set.
Transfer the tin to a wire rack to cool.
<u>7</u> When the bake has cooled for 5
minutes, mark it into 6 x 2.5 cm/2½ x 1 in
bars. Leave until completely cold, then
separate the bars and transfer them to a
wire rack. Dust lightly with icing sugar.
Place the bars on a plate and serve.

COOK'S TIP

Look out for walnut pieces in the
supermarket or health food store.
They are cheaper than walnut halves
and are perfect for this recipe.
Ground almonds would also work
well, but because they are so fine
you need to take care not to over-
process the mixture or they may
become oily.

CHOCOLATE, DATE AND ORANGE BARS

Make the base as in the main recipe,
but substitute hazelnuts for the
walnuts. Roast the hazelnuts briefly
in a hot oven or under the grill, rub
off the skins using a clean, dry
napkin or tea towel, then grind them
with the sugar in a food processor.
Complete the base and bake it as
described, then set it aside.
Make the topping. Mix 225g/8oz/2
cups of sugar-rolled dates,
75g/3oz/6 tbsp butter and
120ml/4fl oz/½ cup water in a
saucepan. Simmer, stirring
occasionally, until the butter has
dissolved and the dates have broken
down to form a pulp. Stir in
50g/2oz/⅓ cup soft light brown
sugar until dissolved. Remove
the pan from the heat and beat in
the grated rind of 1 orange,
with 30ml/2 tbsp orange juice.
Allow to cool.
Beat 175g/6oz/1½ cups self-raising
flour and 1 egg into the date
mixture, then spread the topping
evenly over the hazelnut base. Bake
in a preheated oven at 180°C/
350°F/Gas 4 for 30 minutes. Cool in
the tin, loosen around the edges with
a knife then turn out so that the
hazelnut base is now uppermost.
Glaze with 150g/5oz melted
chocolate. Cut into bars when set.

CHOCOLATE AND COCONUT SLICES

MAKES 24

175g / 6oz digestive biscuits
115g / 4oz / 1 cup walnuts
50g / 2oz / ¼ cup caster sugar
pinch of salt
115g / 4oz / ½ cup butter or margarine, melted
75g / 3oz / 1 cup desiccated coconut
250g / 9oz / 1½ cups plain chocolate chips
250ml / 8fl oz / 1 cup sweetened condensed milk

<u>1</u> Place the digestive biscuits in a paper bag, fold the top over so that the bag is sealed and use a rolling pin to crush the biscuits into coarse crumbs. Chop the walnuts into small pieces, and set aside.

<u>2</u> Preheat oven to 180°C/350°F/Gas 4. Put a baking sheet inside to heat up.

<u>3</u> In a bowl, combine the crushed biscuits, sugar, salt and melted butter or margarine. Press the mixture evenly over the base of an ungreased 33 x 23 cm/ 13 x 9 in baking dish.

<u>4</u> Sprinkle the coconut over the biscuit base, then scatter over the chocolate chips. Pour the condensed milk evenly over the chocolate. Sprinkle the walnuts on top. Place on the hot baking sheet and bake for 30 minutes. Turn out on a wire rack and allow to cool. When cold, cut into slices.

WHITE CHOCOLATE MACADAMIA SLICES

MAKES 16

150g/5oz/1¼ cups macadamia nuts,
blanched almonds or hazelnuts
400g/14oz white chocolate, broken into
squares
115g/4oz/½ cup ready-to-eat dried apricots
75g/3oz/6 tbsp unsalted butter
5ml/1 tsp vanilla essence
3 eggs
150g/5oz/scant 1 cup light muscovado sugar
115g/4oz/1 cup self-raising flour

1 Preheat oven to 190°C/375°F/Gas 5.
Lightly grease two 20 cm/8 in round
sandwich cake tins and line the base of
each with greaseproof paper or non-stick
baking paper.

2 Roughly chop the nuts and half the
white chocolate, making sure that the
pieces are more or less the same size,
then use scissors to cut the apricots to
similar size pieces.

3 In a heatproof bowl over a saucepan of
barely simmering water, melt the
remaining white chocolate with the
butter. Remove from the heat and stir in
the vanilla essence.

4 Whisk the eggs and sugar together in a
mixing bowl until thick and pale, then
pour in the melted chocolate mixture,
whisking constantly.

5 Sift the flour over the mixture and fold
it in evenly. Finally, stir in the nuts,
chopped white chocolate and chopped
dried apricots.

6 Spoon into the tins and level the tops.
Bake for 30–35 minutes or until the top
is firm and crusty. Cool in the tins before
cutting each cake into 8 slices.

MARBLED BROWNIES

MAKES 24

*225g/8oz plain chocolate, chopped into
small pieces*
75g/3oz/6 tbsp butter, diced
4 eggs
300g/11oz/scant 1½ cups granulated sugar
150g/5oz/1¼ cups plain flour
2.5ml/½ tsp salt
5ml/1 tsp baking powder
10ml/2 tsp vanilla essence
115g/4oz/1 cup walnuts, chopped

FOR THE PLAIN MIXTURE

50g/2oz/¼ cup butter, at room temperature
175g/6oz/¾ cup cream cheese
75g/3oz/6 tbsp granulated sugar
2 eggs
25g/1oz/¼ cup plain flour
5ml/1 tsp vanilla essence

<u>1</u> Preheat oven to 180°C/350°F/Gas 4.
Line a 33 x 23 cm/13 x 9 in baking tin
with greaseproof paper or non-stick
baking paper. Grease the paper lightly.

<u>2</u> Melt the chocolate with the butter in a
heatproof bowl over barely simmering
water, stirring constantly until smooth.
Set the mixture aside to cool.

<u>3</u> Meanwhile, beat the eggs in a bowl
until light and fluffy. Gradually add the
sugar and continue beating until blended.
Sift over the flour, salt and baking powder
and fold in gently but thoroughly.

<u>4</u> Stir in the cooled chocolate mixture.
Add the vanilla essence and walnuts.
Measure and set aside 475ml/16fl oz/
2 cups of the chocolate mixture.

<u>5</u> For the plain mixture, cream the butter
and cream cheese in a bowl. Add the
sugar and beat well. Beat in the eggs,
flour and vanilla essence.

<u>6</u> Spread the unmeasured chocolate
mixture in the tin. Pour over the plain
mixture. Drop spoonfuls of the reserved
chocolate mixture on top.

<u>7</u> With a metal palette knife, swirl the
mixtures to marble them. Do not blend
completely. Bake for 35–45 minutes,
until just set. Turn out when cool and cut
into squares for serving.

WHITE CHOCOLATE BROWNIES WITH MILK CHOCOLATE MACADAMIA TOPPING

SERVES 12

115g/4oz/1 cup plain flour
2.5ml/½ tsp baking powder
pinch of salt
175g/6oz fine quality white chocolate,
chopped into small pieces
115g/4oz/½ cup caster sugar
115g/4oz/½ cup unsalted butter, cut into
small pieces
2 eggs, lightly beaten
5ml/1 tsp vanilla essence
175g/6oz plain chocolate chips or plain
chocolate, chopped into small pieces

FOR THE TOPPING

200g/7oz milk chocolate, chopped into
small pieces
175g/6oz/1½ cups unsalted macadamia
nuts, chopped

1 Preheat oven to 180°C/350°F/Gas 4. Grease a 23 cm/9 in springform tin. Sift together the flour, baking powder and salt, set aside.

2 In a medium saucepan over a low heat, melt the white chocolate, sugar and butter until smooth, stirring frequently. Cool slightly, then beat in the eggs and vanilla essence. Stir in the flour mixture until well blended. Stir in the chocolate chips or chopped chocolate. Spread evenly in the prepared tin.

3 Bake for 20–25 minutes, until a cake tester inserted in the cake tin comes out clean; do not over-bake. Remove the cake from the oven and place the tin on a heatproof surface.

4 Sprinkle the chopped milk chocolate evenly over the cake and return it to the oven for 1 minute.

5 Remove the cake from the oven again and gently spread the softened chocolate evenly over the top. Sprinkle with the macadamia nuts and gently press them into the chocolate. Cool on a wire rack for 30 minutes, then chill, for about 1 hour, until set. Run a sharp knife around the side of the tin to loosen, then unclip the side of the springform tin and remove it carefully. Cut into thin wedges.

DOUBLE CHOCOLATE CHIP MUFFINS

MAKES 16

400g/14oz/3½ cups plain flour
15ml/1 tbsp baking powder
30ml/2 tbsp cocoa powder
115g/4oz/⅔ cup dark muscovado sugar
2 eggs
150ml/¼ pint/⅔ cup soured cream
150ml/¼ pint/⅔ cup milk
60ml/4 tbsp sunflower oil
175g/6oz white chocolate, chopped into small pieces
175g/6oz plain chocolate, chopped into small pieces
cocoa powder, for dusting

1 Preheat oven to 180°C/350°F/Gas 4. Place 16 paper muffin cases in muffin tins or deep patty tins. Sift the flour, baking powder and cocoa into a bowl and stir in the sugar. Make a well in the centre.

2 In a separate bowl, beat the eggs with the soured cream, milk and oil, then stir into the well in the dry ingredients. Beat well, gradually incorporating all the surrounding flour mixture to make a thick and creamy batter.

3 Stir the white and plain chocolate pieces into the batter mixture.

4 Spoon the chocolate mixture into the muffin cases, filling them almost to the top. Bake for 25–30 minutes, until well risen and firm to the touch. Cool on a wire rack, then dust the muffins lightly with cocoa powder.

CHOCOLATE WALNUT MUFFINS

MAKES 12

175g / 6oz / ¾ cup unsalted butter
150g / 5oz plain chocolate, chopped into
small pieces
200g / 7oz / scant 1 cup caster sugar
50g / 2oz / ⅓ cup soft dark brown sugar
4 eggs
5ml / 1 tsp vanilla essence
1.5ml / ¼ tsp almond essence
110g / 3¾oz / scant 1 cup plain flour
15ml / 1 tbsp cocoa powder
115g / 4oz / 1 cup walnuts or pecan
nuts, chopped

<u>1</u> Preheat oven to 180°C / 350°F / Gas 4.
Grease a 12-cup muffin tin, or use paper
cases supported in a bun tin.

<u>2</u> Melt the butter with the chocolate in
the top of a double boiler or in a
heatproof bowl set over a saucepan of
simmering water. Transfer to a large
mixing bowl.

<u>3</u> Stir both the sugars into the chocolate
mixture. Mix in the eggs, one at a time,
then add the vanilla and almond essences.

<u>4</u> Sift over the flour and cocoa, fold in,
then stir in the walnuts or pecan nuts.

<u>5</u> Fill the muffin cups or cases almost to
the top and bake for 30–35 minutes, until
a skewer inserted in a muffin comes out
clean but slightly sticky. Leave to stand
for 5 minutes before cooling the muffins
on a rack.

BRIOCHES AU CHOCOLAT

MAKES 12

250g / 9oz / 2¼ cups strong white flour
pinch of salt
30ml / 2 tbsp caster sugar
1 sachet easy-blend dried yeast
3 eggs, beaten, plus extra beaten egg,
for glazing
45ml / 3 tbsp hand-hot milk
115g / 4oz / ½ cup unsalted butter, diced
175g / 6oz plain chocolate, broken into
squares

1 Sift the flour and salt into a large mixing bowl and stir in the sugar and yeast. Make a well in the centre of the mixture and add the eggs and milk.

2 Beat the egg and milk mixture well, gradually incorporating the surrounding dry ingredients to make a fairly soft dough. Turn the dough on to a lightly floured surface and knead well for about 5 minutes, until smooth and elastic, adding a little more flour if necessary.
3 Add the butter to the dough, a few pieces at a time, kneading until each addition is absorbed before adding the next. When all the butter has been incorporated and small bubbles appear in the dough, wrap it in clear film and chill for at least 1 hour. If you intend serving the brioches for breakfast, the dough can be left overnight.

4 Lightly grease 12 individual brioche tins set on a baking sheet or a 12-hole brioche or patty tin. Divide the brioche dough into 12 pieces and shape each into a smooth round. Place a chocolate square in the centre of each round. Bring up the sides of the dough and press the edges firmly together to seal, use a little beaten egg if necessary.
5 Place the brioches, join side down, in the prepared tins. Cover and leave them in a warm place for about 30 minutes or until doubled in size. Preheat oven to 200°C/400°F/Gas 6:

6 Brush the brioches with beaten egg. Bake for 12–15 minutes, until well risen and golden brown. Place on wire racks and leave until they have cooled slightly. They should be served warm and can be made in advance and reheated if necessary. Do not serve straight from the oven, as the chocolate will be very hot.

COOK'S TIP
Brioches freeze well for up to 1 month. Thaw at room temperature, then reheat on baking sheets in a low oven and serve warm, but not hot. For a richer variation serve with melted chocolate drizzled over the top of the brioches.

CHOCOLATE CINNAMON DOUGHNUTS

MAKES 16

500g/1¼lb/5 cups strong plain flour
30ml/2 tbsp cocoa powder
2.5ml/½ tsp salt
1 sachet easy-blend dried yeast
300ml/½ pint/1¼ cups hand-hot milk
40g/1½oz/3 tbsp butter, melted
1 egg, beaten
115g/4oz plain chocolate, broken into
16 pieces
sunflower oil, for deep frying

FOR THE COATING

45ml/3 tbsp caster sugar
15ml/1 tbsp cocoa powder
5ml/1 tsp ground cinnamon

1 Sift the flour, cocoa and salt into a large bowl. Stir in the yeast. Make a well in the centre and add the milk, melted butter and egg. Stir, gradually incorporating the surrounding dry ingredients, to make a soft and pliable dough.

2 Knead the dough on a lightly floured surface for about 5 minutes, until smooth and elastic. Return to the clean bowl, cover with clear film or a clean dry dish towel and leave in a warm place until the dough has doubled in bulk.

3 Knead the dough lightly again, then divide into 16 pieces. Shape each into a round, press a piece of plain chocolate into the centre, then fold the dough over to enclose the filling, pressing firmly to make sure the edges are sealed. Re-shape the doughnuts when sealed, if necessary.

4 Heat the oil for frying to 180°C/350°F or until a cube of dried bread browns in 30–45 seconds. Deep fry the doughnuts in batches. As each doughnut rises and turns golden brown, turn it over to cook the other side. Drain the cooked doughnuts well on kitchen paper.

5 Mix the sugar, cocoa and cinnamon in a shallow bowl. Toss the doughnuts in the mixture to coat them evenly. Pile on a plate and serve warm.

VARIATION

Instead of using a square of plain chocolate to fill each doughnut, try chocolate spread instead. Use about 5ml/1 tsp of the spread for each doughnut. Seal well before frying.

CHOCOLATE ORANGE SPONGE DROPS

MAKES ABOUT 14

2 eggs
50g / 2 oz / ¼ cup caster sugar
2.5ml / ½ tsp grated orange rind
50g / 2oz / ½ cup plain flour
60ml / 4 tbsp finely shredded orange marmalade
40g / 1½oz plain chocolate, chopped into small pieces

1 Preheat oven to 200°C/400°F/Gas 6. Line three baking sheets with baking parchment. Put the eggs and sugar in a large heatproof bowl and whisk over a pan of simmering water until the mixture is thick and pale.

2 Remove the bowl from the pan of water and continue whisking until the mixture is cool. Whisk in the grated orange rind. Sift the flour over the whisked mixture and fold it in gently.

3 Put spoonfuls of the mixture on the baking sheets, spacing them well apart to allow for spreading. The mixture will make 28–30 drops. Bake for about 8 minutes or until the biscuits are golden. Allow them to cool on the baking sheets for a few minutes, then use a spatula to transfer them to a wire rack to cool completely. Sandwich the biscuits together in pairs with the marmalade.

4 Melt the chocolate in a heatproof bowl set over a pan of barely simmering water. Drizzle or pipe the chocolate over the tops of the sponge drops. Leave to set before serving.

SWEETS, TRUFFLES AND DRINKS

CHOCOLATE AND CHERRY COLETTES

MAKES 18–20

*115g/4oz plain dark chocolate, chopped into
small pieces*
*75g/3oz white or milk chocolate, chopped
into small pieces*
25g/1oz/2 tbsp unsalted butter, melted
15ml/1 tbsp Kirsch or brandy
60ml/4 tbsp double cream
*18–20 maraschino cherries or liqueur-soaked
cherries*
milk chocolate curls, to decorate

1 Melt the dark chocolate, then remove it
from the heat. Spoon into 18 20 foil
sweet cases, spread evenly up the sides
with a small brush, then leave the cases in
a cool place until the chocolate has set.

2 Melt the white or milk chocolate with
the butter. Remove from the heat and stir
in the Kirsch or brandy, then the cream.
Cool until the mixture is thick enough to
hold its shape.

3 Carefully peel away the paper from the
chocolate cases. Place one cherry in each
chocolate case. Spoon the white or milk
chocolate cream mixture into a piping
bag fitted with a small star nozzle and
pipe over the cherries until the cases are
full. Top each colette with a generous
swirl, and decorate with milk chocolate
curls. Leave to set before serving.

PEPPERMINT CHOCOLATE STICKS

MAKES ABOUT 80

115g/4oz/½ cup granulated sugar
150ml/¼ pint/⅔ cup water
2.5ml/½ tsp peppermint essence
200g/7oz plain dark chocolate, chopped into
small pieces
60ml/4 tbsp toasted desiccated coconut

1 Lightly oil a large baking sheet. Place the sugar and water in a small, heavy-based saucepan and heat gently, stirring until the sugar has dissolved.
2 Bring to the boil and boil rapidly without stirring until the syrup registers 138°C/280°F on a sugar thermometer. Remove the pan from the heat and stir in the peppermint essence.

3 Pour the mixture on to the greased baking sheet and leave until set.

4 Break up the peppermint mixture into a small bowl and use the end of a rolling pin to crush it into small pieces.
5 Melt the chocolate. Remove from the heat and stir in the mint pieces and desiccated coconut.

6 Lay a 30 x 25cm/12 x 10in sheet of non-stick baking paper on a flat surface. Spread the chocolate mixture over the paper, leaving a narrow border all around, to make a rectangle measuring about 25 x 20cm/10 x 8in. Leave to set. When firm, use a sharp knife to cut into thin sticks, each about 6cm/2½in long.

CHOCOLATE TRUFFLES

MAKES 20 LARGE OR 30 MEDIUM TRUFFLES

250ml/8fl oz/1 cup double cream
275g/10oz fine quality bittersweet or plain chocolate, chopped into small pieces
40g/1½oz/3 tbsp unsalted butter, cut into small pieces
45ml/3 tbsp brandy, whisky or liqueur of own choice
cocoa powder, for dusting (optional)
finely chopped pistachio nuts, to decorate (optional)
400g/14oz bittersweet chocolate, to decorate (optional)

1 Pour the cream into a saucepan. Bring to the boil over a medium heat. Remove from the heat and add the chocolate, all at once. Stir gently until melted. Stir in the butter until melted, then stir in the brandy, whisky or liqueur. Strain into a bowl and cool to room temperature. Cover the mixture with clear film and chill for 4 hours or overnight.

2 Line a large baking sheet with non-stick baking paper. Using a small ice cream scoop, melon baller or tablespoon, scrape up the mixture into 20 large balls or 30 medium balls and place on the lined baking sheet. Dip the scoop or spoon in cold water from time to time, to prevent the mixture from sticking.

3 If dusting with cocoa powder, sift a thick layer of cocoa on to a dish or pie plate. Roll the truffles in the cocoa, rounding them between the palms of your hands. (Dust your hands with cocoa to prevent the truffles from sticking.) Do not worry if the truffles are not perfectly round as an irregular shape looks more authentic. Alternatively, roll the truffles in very finely chopped pistachios. Chill on the paper-lined baking sheet until firm. Keep in the fridge for up to 10 days or freeze for up to 2 months.

4 If coating with chocolate, do not roll the truffles in cocoa, but freeze them for 1 hour. For perfect results, temper the chocolate. Alternatively, simply melt it in a heatproof bowl over a saucepan of barely simmering water. Using a fork, dip the truffles, one at a time, into the melted chocolate, tapping the fork on the edge of the bowl to shake off excess. Place on a baking sheet, lined with non-stick baking paper. If the chocolate begins to thicken, reheat it gently until smooth. Chill the truffles until set.

MALT WHISKY TRUFFLES

MAKES 25–30

*200g/7oz plain dark chocolate, chopped into
small pieces
150ml/¼ pint/⅔ cup double cream
45ml/3 tbsp malt whisky
115g/4oz/¾ cup icing sugar
cocoa powder, for coating*

1 Melt the chocolate in a heatproof bowl over a saucepan of simmering water, stir until smooth, then cool slightly.

2 Using a wire whisk, whip the cream with the whisky in a bowl until thick enough to hold its shape.

3 Stir in the melted chocolate and icing sugar, mixing evenly, then leave until firm enough to handle.

4 Dust your hands with cocoa powder and shape the mixture into bite-size balls. Coat in cocoa powder and pack into pretty cases or boxes. Store in the fridge for up to 3–4 days if necessary.

TRUFFLE-FILLED EASTER EGG

MAKES 1 LARGE, HOLLOW EASTER EGG
350g / 12oz plain couverture chocolate,
tempered, or plain, milk or white chocolate,
melted
Chocolate Truffles

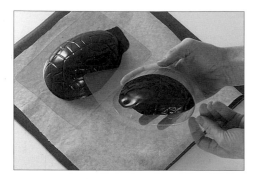

1 Line a small baking sheet with non-stick baking paper. Using a small ladle or spoon, pour in enough melted chocolate to coat both halves of an Easter egg mould. Tilt the half-moulds slowly to coat the sides completely; pour any excess chocolate back into the bowl. Set the half-moulds, open side down, on the prepared baking sheet and leave for 1–2 minutes until just set.

2 Apply a second coat of chocolate and chill for 1–3 minutes more, until set. Repeat a third time, then replace the moulds on the baking sheet and chill for at least 1 hour or until the chocolate has set completely. (Work quickly to avoid having to temper the chocolate again; untempered chocolate can be reheated if it hardens.)

3 To remove the set chocolate, place a half-mould, open side up, on a board. Carefully trim any drops of chocolate from the edge of the mould. Gently insert the point of a small knife between the chocolate and the mould to break the air lock. Repeat with the second mould.

4 Holding the mould open side down, squeeze firmly to release the egg half. Repeat with the other half and chill, loosely covered. (Do not touch the chocolate surface with your fingers, as they will leave prints.) Reserve any melted chocolate to reheat for "glue".

5 To assemble the egg, hold one half of the egg with a piece of folded kitchen paper or foil and fill with small truffles. If necessary, use the remaining melted chocolate as "glue". Spread a small amount on to the rim of the egg half and, holding the empty egg half with a piece of kitchen paper or foil, press it on to the filled half, making sure the rims are aligned and carefully joined.

6 Hold for several seconds, then prop up the egg with the folded paper or foil and chill to set. If you like, decorate the egg with ribbons or Easter decorations.

CHOCOLATE ALMOND TORRONNE

MAKES ABOUT 20 SLICES

*115g/4oz plain dark chocolate, chopped into
small pieces*
50g/2oz/¼ cup unsalted butter
1 egg white
115g/4oz/½ cup caster sugar
75g/3oz/¾ cup chopped toasted almonds
50g/2oz/½ cup ground almonds
75ml/5 tbsp chopped candied peel

FOR THE COATING
*175g/6oz white chocolate, chopped into small
pieces*
25g/1oz/2 tbsp unsalted butter
115g/4oz/1 cup flaked almonds, toasted

<u>1</u> Melt the chocolate with the butter in a
heatproof bowl over a saucepan of barely
simmering water until smooth.

<u>2</u> In a clean, grease-free bowl, whisk the
egg white with the sugar until stiff.
Gradually beat in the melted chocolate
mixture, then stir in the toasted almonds,
ground almonds and peel.
<u>3</u> Tip the mixture on to a large sheet of
non-stick baking paper and shape into a
thick roll.

<u>4</u> As the mixture cools, use the paper to
press the roll firmly into a triangular
shape. When you are satisfied with the
shape, twist the paper over the triangular
roll and chill until completely set.
<u>5</u> Make the coating. Melt the white
chocolate with the butter in a heatproof
bowl over a saucepan of simmering water.
Unwrap the chocolate roll and with a
clean knife spread the white chocolate
quickly over the surface. Press the flaked
almonds in a thin even coating over the
chocolate, working quickly before the
chocolate sets.
<u>6</u> Chill the coated chocolate roll again
until firm, then cut the torronne into
fairly thin slices to serve. Torronne is
ideal to finish a dinner party.

DOUBLE CHOCOLATE-DIPPED FRUIT

MAKES 24 COATED PIECES

fruits – about 24 pieces (strawberries, cherries, orange segments, large seedless grapes, physalis (Cape gooseberries), kumquats, stoned prunes, stoned dates, dried apricots, dried peaches or dried pears)
115g/4oz white chocolate, chopped into small pieces
115g/4oz bittersweet or plain chocolate, chopped into small pieces

1 Clean and prepare fruits; wipe strawberries with a soft cloth or brush gently with pastry brush. Wash firm-skinned fruits such as cherries and grapes and dry well. Peel and leave whole or cut up any other fruits being used.

CHOCOLATE PEPPERMINT CREAMS

1 egg white
90ml/6 tbsp double cream
5ml/1 tsp peppermint essence
675g/1½lb/5½ cups icing sugar, plus extra for dusting
few drops of green food colouring
175g/6oz plain chocolate, chopped into small pieces

1 Beat the egg white lightly in a bowl. Mix in the cream and peppermint essence, then gradually add the icing sugar to make a firm, pliable dough. Work in 1–2 drops of green food colouring (apply it from a cocktail stick if you are anxious about adding too much colour) until the dough is an even, pale green.
2 On a surface dusted with icing sugar, roll out the dough to a thickness of about 1cm/½in. Stamp out 4cm/1½in rounds of squares and place on a baking sheet lined with non-stick baking paper. Leave to dry for at least 8 hours, turning once.
3 Melt the chocolate in a bowl over barely simmering water. Allow to cool slightly. Spread chocolate over the top of each peppermint cream, and place them on fresh sheets of non-stick paper. Chill until set.

2 Melt the white chocolate. Remove from the heat and cool to tepid (about 29°C/84°F), stirring frequently. Line a baking sheet with non-stick baking paper. Holding each fruit by the stem or end and at an angle, dip about two-thirds of the fruit into the chocolate. Allow the excess to drip off and place on the baking sheet. Chill the fruits for about 20 minutes until the chocolate sets.

3 Melt the bittersweet or plain chocolate, stirring frequently until smooth.

4 Remove the chocolate from the heat and cool to just below body temperature, about 30°C/86°F. Take each white chocolate-coated fruit in turn from the baking sheet and, holding by the stem or end and at the opposite angle, dip the bottom third of each piece into the dark chocolate, creating a chevron effect. Set on the baking sheet. Chill for 15 minutes or until set. Before serving, allow the fruit to stand at room temperature 10–15 minutes before serving.

CHOCOLATE-COATED NUT BRITTLE

MAKES 20–24 PIECES

115g/4oz/1 cup mixed pecan nuts and whole almonds
115g/4oz/½ cup caster sugar
60ml/4 tbsp water
200g/7oz plain dark chocolate, chopped into small pieces

1 Lightly grease a baking sheet with butter or oil. Mix the nuts, sugar and water in a heavy-based saucepan. Place the pan over a gentle heat, stirring until all the sugar has dissolved.

2 Bring to the boil, then lower the heat to moderate and cook until the mixture turns a rich golden brown and registers 155°C/310°F on a sugar thermometer. If you do not have a sugar thermometer, test the syrup by adding a few drops to a cup of iced water. The mixture should solidify to a very brittle mass.

CHOCOLATE-COATED HAZELNUTS

Roast about 225g/8oz/2 cups hazelnuts in the oven or under the grill. Allow to cool. Melt the chocolate in a heatproof bowl over a pan of barely simmering water. Remove from the heat, but leave the bowl over the water so that the chocolate remains liquid. Have ready about 30 paper sweet cases, arranged on baking sheets. Add the roasted hazelnuts to the melted chocolate and stir to coat. Using two spoons, carefully scoop up a cluster of two or three chocolate-coated nuts. Carefully transfer the cluster to a paper sweet case. Leave the nut clusters in a cool place until set.

3 Quickly remove the pan from the heat and tip the mixture on to the prepared baking sheet, spreading it evenly. Leave until completely cold and hard.

4 Break the nut brittle into bite-size pieces. Melt the chocolate and dip the pieces to half-coat them. Leave on a sheet of non-stick baking paper to set.

CHOCOLATE NUT CLUSTERS

MAKES ABOUT 30

525ml/21fl oz/2½ cups double cream
25g/1oz/2 tbsp unsalted butter, cut into small pieces
350ml/12fl oz/1½ cups golden syrup
200g/7oz/scant 1 cup granulated sugar
75g/3oz/⅓ cup light brown sugar
pinch of salt
15ml/1 tbsp vanilla essence
350g/12oz/3 cups combination of hazelnuts, pecans, walnuts, brazil nuts and unsalted peanuts
400g/14oz plain chocolate, chopped into small pieces
15g/½oz/1 tbsp white vegetable fat

1 Lightly brush two baking sheets with vegetable oil. In a large heavy-based saucepan over a medium heat, cook the cream, butter, golden syrup, sugars and salt, stirring occasionally for about 3 minutes, until the sugars dissolve and the butter melts.

2 Bring to the boil and continue cooking, stirring frequently for about 1 hour, until the caramel reaches 119°C/238°F on a sugar thermometer, or until a small amount of caramel dropped into a cup of iced water forms a hard ball.

3 Plunge the bottom of the pan into cold water to stop cooking. Cool slightly, then stir in the vanilla essence.

4 Stir the nuts into the caramel until well coated. Using an oiled tablespoon, drop spoonfuls of nut mixture on to the prepared sheets, about 2.5cm/1in apart. If the mixture hardens, return to the heat to soften. Chill the clusters for 30 minutes until firm and cold, or leave in a cool place until hardened.

5 Using a metal palette knife, transfer the clusters to a wire rack placed over a baking sheet to catch drips. In a medium saucepan, over a low heat, melt the chocolate with the white vegetable fat, stirring until smooth. Set aside to cool slightly.

6 Spoon chocolate over each cluster, being sure to cover completely.

7 Place on a wire rack over a baking sheet. Allow to set for 2 hours until hardened. Store in an airtight container.

CHOCOLATE FUDGE TRIANGLES

MAKES ABOUT 48 TRIANGLES

600g/1lb 5oz fine quality white chocolate, chopped into small pieces
375g/13oz can sweetened condensed milk
15ml/1 tbsp vanilla essence
7.5ml/1½ tsp lemon juice
pinch of salt
175g/6oz/1½ cups hazelnuts or pecan nuts, chopped (optional)
175g/6oz plain chocolate, chopped into small pieces
40g/1½oz/3 tbsp unsalted butter, cut into small pieces
50g/2oz bittersweet chocolate, for drizzling

1 Line a 20cm/8in square baking tin with foil. Brush the foil lightly with oil. In a saucepan over low heat, melt the white chocolate and condensed milk until smooth, stirring frequently. Remove from the heat and stir in the vanilla essence, lemon juice and salt. Stir in the nuts if using. Spread half the mixture in the tin. Chill for 15 minutes.

2 In a saucepan over low heat, melt the plain chocolate and butter until smooth, stirring frequently. Remove from the heat, cool slightly, then pour over the chilled white layer and chill for 15 minutes until set.

3 Gently re-heat the remaining white chocolate mixture and pour over the set chocolate layer. Smooth the top, then chill for 2–4 hours until set.

4 Using the foil as a guide, remove the fudge from the pan and turn it on to a cutting board. Lift off the foil and use a sharp knife to cut the fudge into 24 squares. Cut each square into a triangle. Melt the bittersweet chocolate in a heatproof bowl over a pan of barely simmering water. Cool slightly, then drizzle over the triangles.

EASY CHOCOLATE HAZELNUT FUDGE

MAKES 16 SQUARES

150ml/¼ pint/⅔ cup evaporated milk
350g/12oz/1½ cups sugar
large pinch of salt
50g/2oz/½ cup hazelnuts, halved
350g/12oz/2 cups plain chocolate chips

1 Generously grease a 20cm/8in square cake tin.

2 Place the evaporated milk, sugar and salt in a heavy-based saucepan. Bring to the boil over a medium heat, stirring constantly. Lower the heat and simmer gently, stirring, for about 5 minutes.

3 Remove the pan from the heat and add the hazelnuts and chocolate chips. Stir gently with a metal spoon until the chocolate has completely melted.

4 Quickly pour the fudge mixture into the prepared tin and spread evenly. Leave to cool and set.

5 When the chocolate hazelnut fudge has set, cut it into 2.5cm/1in squares. Store in an airtight container, separating the layers with greaseproof paper or non-stick baking paper.

TWO-TONE FUDGE

Make the Easy Chocolate Hazelnut Fudge and spread it in a 23cm/9in square cake tin, to make a slightly thinner layer than for the main recipe. While it is cooling, make a batch of plain fudge, substituting white chocolate drops for the plain chocolate chips and leaving out the hazelnuts. Let the plain fudge cool slightly before pouring it carefully over the dark chocolate layer. Use a palette knife or slim metal spatula to spread the plain layer to the corners, then set aside to set as before. Cut into squares.

RICH CHOCOLATE PISTACHIO FUDGE

MAKES 36

250g/9oz/generous 1 cup granulated sugar
375g/13oz can sweetened condensed milk
50g/2oz/¼ cup unsalted butter
5ml/1 tsp vanilla essence
115g/4oz plain dark chocolate, grated
75g/3oz/¾ cup pistachio nuts, almonds
or hazelnuts

CHOCOLATE AND MARSHMALLOW FUDGE

25g/1oz/2 tbsp butter
350g/12oz/1½ cups granulated sugar
175ml/6fl oz/¾ cup evaporated milk
pinch of salt
115g/4oz/2 cups white mini marshmallows
225g/8oz /1¼ cups chocolate chips
5ml/1 tsp vanilla essence
115g/4oz/½ cup chopped walnuts
(optional)

1 Generously grease an 18cm/7 in cake tin. Mix the butter, sugar, evaporated milk and salt in a heavy-based saucepan. Stir over a medium heat until the sugar has dissolved, then bring to the boil and cook for 3–5 minutes or until thickened, stirring all the time.
2 Remove the pan from the heat and beat in the marshmallows and chocolate chips until dissolved. Beat in the vanilla essence. Scrape the mixture into the prepared cake tin and press it evenly into the corners, using a metal palette knife. Level the surface.
3 If using the walnuts, sprinkle them over the fudge and press them in to the surface. Set the fudge aside to cool. Before it has set completely, mark it into squares with a sharp knife. Chill until firm before cutting the fudge up and serving it.

1 Grease a 19cm/7½in square cake tin and line with non-stick baking paper. Mix the sugar, condensed milk and butter in a heavy-based pan. Heat gently, stirring occasionally, until the sugar has dissolved completely and the mixture is smooth.
2 Bring the mixture to the boil, stirring occasionally, and boil until it registers 116°C/240°F on a sugar thermometer or until a small amount of the mixture dropped into a cup of iced water forms a soft ball.
3 Remove the pan from the heat and beat in the vanilla essence, chocolate and nuts. Beat vigorously until the mixture is smooth and creamy.

4 Pour the mixture into the prepared cake tin and spread evenly. Leave until just set, then mark into squares. Leave to set completely before cutting into squares and removing from the tin. Store in an airtight container in a cool place.

TRUFFLE-FILLED FILO CUPS

MAKES ABOUT 24 CUPS

3–6 sheets fresh or thawed frozen filo pastry,
depending on size
40g / 1½ oz / 3 tbsp unsalted butter, melted
sugar, for sprinkling
pared strips of lemon zest, to decorate

FOR THE CHOCOLATE TRUFFLE
MIXTURE

250ml / 8fl oz / 1 cup double cream
225g / 8oz bittersweet or plain chocolate,
chopped into small pieces
50g / 2oz / ¼ cup unsalted butter, cut into
small pieces
30ml / 2 tbsp brandy or liqueur

1 Prepare the truffle mixture. In a saucepan over a medium heat, bring the cream to a boil. Remove from the heat and add the pieces of chocolate, stirring until melted. Beat in the butter and add the brandy or liqueur. Strain into a bowl and chill for 1 hour until thick.

2 Preheat oven to 200°C/400°F/Gas 6. Grease a 12-hole bun tray. Cut the filo sheets into 6cm/2½ in squares. Cover with a damp dish towel. Place one square on a work surface. Brush lightly with melted butter, turn over and brush the other side. Sprinkle with a pinch of sugar. Butter another square and place it over the first at an angle; sprinkle with sugar. Butter a third square and place over the first two, unevenly, so the corners form an uneven edge. Press the layered square into one of the holes in the bun tray.

3 Continue to fill the tray, working quickly so that the filo does not have time to dry out. Bake the filo cups for 4–6 minutes, until golden. Cool for 10 minutes on the bun tray then carefully transfer to a wire rack and cool completely.

4 Stir the chocolate mixture; it should be just thick enough to pipe. Spoon the mixture into a piping bag fitted with a medium star nozzle and pipe a swirl into each filo cup. Decorate each with tiny strips of lemon zest.

MEXICAN HOT CHOCOLATE

SERVES 4

1 litre / 1¾ pints / 4 cups milk
1 cinnamon stick
2 whole cloves
115g / 4oz plain dark chocolate, chopped into
small pieces
2–3 drops of almond essence

1 Heat the milk gently with the spices in a saucepan until almost boiling, then stir in the plain chocolate over a moderate heat until melted.

2 Strain into a blender, add the almond essence and whizz on high speed for about 30 seconds until frothy. Alternatively, whisk the mixture with a hand-held electric mixer or wire whisk.

3 Pour into warmed heatproof glasses and serve immediately.

WHITE HOT CHOCOLATE

SERVES 4

1.75 litres / 3 pints / 7½ cups milk
175g / 6oz white chocolate, chopped into
small pieces
10ml / 2 tsp coffee powder
10ml / 2 tsp orange-flavoured liqueur
(optional)
whipped cream and ground cinnamon, to serve

1 Pour the milk into a large heavy-based saucepan and heat until almost boiling. As soon as bubbles form around the edge of the pan remove the milk from the heat.

2 Add the white chocolate, coffee powder and orange-flavoured liqueur, if using. Stir until all the chocolate has melted and the mixture is smooth.

3 Pour the hot chocolate into four mugs. Top each with a swirl or spoonful of whipped cream and a sprinkling of ground cinnamon. Serve immediately.

ICED MINT AND CHOCOLATE COOLER

SERVES 4

60ml/4 tbsp drinking chocolate
400ml/14fl oz/1⅔ cups chilled milk
150ml/¼ pint/⅔ cup natural yogurt
2.5ml/½ tsp peppermint essence
4 scoops of chocolate ice cream
mint leaves and chocolate shapes, to decorate

1 Place the drinking chocolate in a small pan and stir in about 120ml/4fl oz/½ cup of the milk. Heat gently, stirring, until almost boiling, then remove the pan from the heat.

2 Pour the hot chocolate milk into a heatproof bowl or large jug and whisk in the remaining milk. Add the natural yogurt and peppermint essence and whisk again.

3 Pour the mixture into four tall glasses, filling them no more than three-quarters full. Top each drink with a scoop of ice cream. Decorate with mint leaves and chocolate shapes. Serve immediately.

CHOCOLATE VANILLA COOLER

Make the drink as in the main recipe, but use single cream instead of the natural yogurt and 5ml/1 tsp natural vanilla essence instead of the peppermint essence.

MOCHA COOLER

Make the drink as in the main recipe, but dissolve the chocolate in 120ml/4fl oz/½ cup strong black coffee, and reduce the milk to 300ml/½ pint/1¼ cups. Use cream instead of yogurt and leave the essence out.

IRISH CHOCOLATE VELVET

SERVES 4

250ml/8fl oz/1 cup double cream
400ml/14fl oz/1⅔ cups milk
115g/4oz milk chocolate, chopped into small pieces
30ml/2 tbsp cocoa powder
60ml/4 tbsp Irish whiskey
whipped cream, for topping
chocolate curls, to decorate

1 Using a hand-held electric mixer, whip half the cream in a bowl until it is thick enough to hold its shape.

2 Place the milk and chocolate in a saucepan and heat gently, stirring, until the chocolate has melted.

3 Whisk in the cocoa, then bring to the boil. Remove from the heat and stir in the remaining cream and the Irish whiskey.

4 Pour quickly into four warmed heatproof mugs or glasses and top each serving with a generous spoonful of the whipped cream, then the chocolate curls. Serve with Peppermint Sticks for extra indulgence.

SAUCES, FROSTINGS AND ICINGS

SIMPLE BUTTERCREAM

MAKES ABOUT 350G/12OZ

75g/3oz butter or soft margarine
225g/8oz/1½ cups icing sugar
5ml/1 tsp vanilla essence
10–15ml/2–3 tsp milk

1 If using butter, allow it to come to room temperature so that it can easily be creamed. Sift the icing sugar. Put the butter or margarine in a bowl. Add about a quarter of the icing sugar and beat with a hand-held electric mixer until fluffy.

2 Using a metal spoon, add the remaining sifted icing sugar, a little at a time, beating well with the electric mixer after each addition. Icing sugar is so fine that if you add too much of it at one time, it tends to fly out of the bowl.

3 Beat in 5ml/1 tsp of the milk. The mixture should be light and creamy, with a spreadable consistency. Add the vanilla essence, then more milk if necessary, but not too much, or it will be too sloppy to draw into peaks. Use as a filling and/or topping on layer cakes and cupcakes.

CHOCOLATE BUTTERCREAM

ENOUGH TO FILL A 20CM/8IN ROUND LAYER CAKE

75g/3oz/6 tbsp unsalted butter or margarine, softened
175g/6oz/1 cup icing sugar
15ml/1 tbsp cocoa powder
2.5ml/½ tsp vanilla essence

1 Place all the ingredients in a large bowl.

2 Beat well to a smooth spreadable consistency.

VARIATIONS

Coffee Buttercream: Stir 10ml/2 tsp instant coffee into 15ml/1 tbsp boiling water. Beat into the icing instead of the milk.
Mocha Buttercream: Stir 5ml/1 tsp cocoa powder into 10ml/2 tsp boiling water. Beat into the icing. Add a little coffee essence.
Orange Buttercream: Use orange juice instead of the milk and vanilla essence, and add 10ml/2 tsp finely grated orange rind. Omit the rind if using the icing for piping.

WHITE CHOCOLATE FROSTING

ENOUGH TO COVER A 20CM/8IN ROUND CAKE

175g/6oz white chocolate, chopped into small pieces
75g/3oz/6 tbsp unsalted butter
115g/4oz/¾ cup icing sugar
90ml/6 tbsp double cream

1 Melt the chocolate with the butter in a heatproof bowl over a saucepan of barely simmering water. Remove the bowl from the heat and beat in the icing sugar, a little at a time, using a wire whisk.

2 Whip the cream in a separate bowl until it just holds its shape, then beat into the chocolate mixture. Allow the mixture to cool, stirring occasionally, until it begins to hold its shape. Use immediately.

COOK'S TIP

White chocolate frosting is a rich frosting suitable for a dark chocolate sponge without a filling. Use a palette knife to form peaks for an attractive finish.

SATIN CHOCOLATE ICING

MAKES 225G/8OZ

*175g/6oz plain or bittersweet
chocolate, chopped into small pieces
150ml/¼ pint/⅔ cup double cream
2.5ml/½ tsp instant coffee powder*

COOK'S TIP
Do not touch the icing once it has
hardened or the attractive satin finish
will be spoilt. Cakes covered with
this icing need little by way of
decoration, but half-dipped cherries
look very effective.

1 Put the chocolate, cream and coffee in a
small heavy-based saucepan. Place the
cake to be iced on a wire rack over a
baking sheet or tray.

2 Place the saucepan over a very low heat
and stir the mixture with a wooden spoon
until all the pieces of plain or bittersweet
chocolate have melted and the mixture is
smooth and evenly blended.

3 Remove from the heat and immediately
pour the icing over the cake, letting it run
down the sides slowly to coat it
completely. Spread the icing with a
palette knife or slim spatula as necessary,
working quickly before the icing has time
to thicken.

CHOCOLATE FONDANT
**ENOUGH TO COVER AND DECORATE
A 23CM/9IN ROUND CAKE**

*350g/12oz plain chocolate, chopped into
small pieces
60ml/4 tbsp liquid glucose
2 egg whites
900g/2lb/7 cups icing sugar*

1 Put the chocolate and glucose in a
heatproof bowl. Place over a
saucepan of barely simmering water
and leave to melt, stirring the
mixture occasionally. When it is
smooth, remove the bowl from the
heat and cool slightly.
2 In a clean, grease-free bowl, whisk the
egg whites with a hand-held electric
mixer until soft peaks form, then stir
into the chocolate mixture with about
45ml/3 tbsp of the icing sugar.
3 Continue to beat the icing,
gradually adding enough of the
remaining icing sugar to make a stiff
paste. Wrap the fondant in clear film
if not using immediately.

FUDGE FROSTING

MAKES 350G/12OZ

50g/2oz plain chocolate, chopped into
small pieces
225g/8oz/2 cups icing sugar, sifted
50g/2oz/¼ cup butter or margarine
45ml/3 tbsp milk or single cream
15ml/1 tbsp vanilla essence

COOK'S TIP

When you have covered the cake
with the frosting, use the back of a
spoon or the tines of a fork to swirl
the fudge frosting and create an
attractive pattern on the cake, but do
this quickly, as it sets very fast.

1 Put the chocolate, icing sugar, butter or
margarine, milk or cream and vanilla
essence in a heavy-based saucepan.
2 Stir over a very low heat until the
chocolate and butter or margarine melt.
Turn off the heat, stir until smooth.

3 Beat the icing frequently as it cools until
it thickens sufficiently to use for
spreading or piping. Use immediately and
work quickly once it has reached the right
consistency. This is a popular frosting and
can be used for many kinds of cakes.

CHOCOLATE FUDGE SAUCE

SERVES 6
150ml/¼ pint/⅔ cup double cream
50g/2oz/¼ cup butter
50g/2oz/¼ cup vanilla sugar
175g/6oz plain chocolate, chopped into
small pieces
30ml/2 tbsp brandy

1 Heat the cream with the butter and sugar in a bowl over a saucepan of barely simmering water. Stir until smooth, then leave to cool.

2 Add the chocolate to the cream mixture. Stir over simmering water until it is melted and thoroughly combined.

3 Stir in the brandy a little at a time, then cool to room temperature.

CHOCOLATE GANACHE
ENOUGH TO COVER A 23CM/9IN
ROUND CAKE
225g/8oz plain chocolate, chopped into
small pieces
250ml/8fl oz/1 cup double cream

Melt the chocolate with the cream in a saucepan over a low heat. Pour into a bowl, leave to cool, then whisk until the mixture begins to hold its shape.

WHITE CHOCOLATE AND ORANGE SAUCE

SERVES 6
150ml/¼ pint/⅔ cup double cream
50g/2oz/¼ cup butter
45ml/3 tbsp caster sugar
175g/6oz white chocolate, chopped into
small pieces
30ml/2 tbsp orange-flavoured liqueur
finely grated rind of 1 orange

COOK'S TIP
Serve with ice cream, or with hot waffles or fresh crêpes.

1 Pour the cream into a heavy-based saucepan. Cut the butter into cubes and add it to the pan, with the sugar. Heat gently, stirring the mixture occasionally until the butter has melted.

2 Add the chocolate to the cream. Stir over a very low heat until it is melted and thoroughly combined.
3 Stir in the orange rind, then add the liqueur a little at a time. Leave to cool.

BITTERSWEET CHOCOLATE SAUCE

QUICK CHOCOLATE SAUCE
MAKES 225ML/8FL OZ/1 CUP
150ml/¼ pint/⅔ cup double cream
15ml/1 tbsp caster sugar
*150g/5oz plain chocolate, chopped into
small pieces*
*30ml/2 tbsp dark rum or whisky
(optional)*

1 Bring the cream and sugar to the
boil. Remove from the heat, add the
chocolate and stir until melted. Stir
in the rum or whisky.
2 Pour the chocolate sauce into a jar.
When cool, cover and store for up to
10 days. Reheat by standing the jar in
a saucepan of simmering water, or
remove the lid and microwave on
High power for 2 minutes. Stir
before serving.

MAKES ABOUT 350ML/12FL OZ
45ml/3 tbsp granulated sugar
120ml/4fl oz/½ cup water
*175g/6oz bittersweet chocolate, chopped into
small pieces*
25g/1oz/2 tbsp unsalted butter, diced
60–90ml/4–6 tbsp single cream
2.5ml/½ tsp vanilla essence

1 Combine the sugar and water in a
heavy-based saucepan. Bring to the boil
over a medium heat, stirring constantly
until all the sugar has dissolved.

2 Add the chocolate and butter to the
syrup, stir with a wooden spoon, then
remove the pan from the heat and
continue to stir until smooth.

3 Stir in the single cream and vanilla
essence. Serve the sauce warm, over
vanilla ice cream, profiteroles, poached
pears or crêpes.

GLOSSY CHOCOLATE SAUCE

SERVES 6
115g/4oz/½ cup caster sugar
60ml/4 tbsp water
*175g/6oz plain chocolate, chopped into
small pieces*
25g/1oz/2 tbsp unsalted butter
30ml/2 tbsp brandy or orange juice

COOK'S TIP
Any of these sauces would make a
chocolate fondue, with fruit and
dessert biscuits as dippers.

1 Place the caster sugar and water in a
heavy-based saucepan and heat gently,
stirring occasionally with a wooden spoon
until all the sugar has dissolved.

2 Stir in the chocolate until melted, then
add the butter in the same way. Do not
allow the sauce to boil. Stir in the brandy
or orange juice and serve warm.

INDEX